ROSES FOR GRAMSCI

Roses for Gramsci

ANDY MERRIFIELD

MONTHLY REVIEW PRESS

New York

Library of Congress Cataloging-in-Publication Data
available from the publisher.

ISBN: 978-168590-104-2 cloth

*Photo on page 42 by Tatiana Morici, used with permission. All other photos
courtesy of the author.*

Typeset in Bulmer MT

Monthly Review Press | New York
www.monthlyreview.org

5 4 3 2 1

In memory of John Berger, 1926–2017

In memory of John Berger, 1926–2017

1

OBLIGATION

I'm sitting at the bar of Blackmarket Hall in Rome, a trendy food and drink hangout not far from my new home in Monti. It's Friday night and the joint is jumping. I've had a couple of glasses of wine, and a whole world spins around in my head. I'm conscious that I've been inactive for a few months now, feeling exhausted, a bit overwhelmed by the practical chores my recent move from Britain necessitated. My brain felt dead. Yet sitting here, amid a crowded scene of noisy, young revelers, listening to seventies funk music boom out, tunes I remember first time around, I knew I had to try to do something creative again soon.

The feeling, a kind of urgency of the moment, was prompted by what I was reading. I had with me a copy of John Berger's book of essays, *The White Bird*, from the mid-1980s, taking it along to offset my aloneness. A book is always a good cover for the solitary person in public, an effective disguise. I was in awe at how good these pieces were. *White Bird*'s most famous essay is "The Moment of Cubism," but tonight, I guess I was having my "Moment of John Berger." I remember John once telling me—or else I'd read it somewhere—that he'd hated *White Bird*; when it first appeared, he threw it across the room in disgust, launched it like a missile. He never thought it any good. My God, what could he have been thinking? Was he talking about its form or content? Its content, after all, while previously published material, is as brilliant as I recall, maybe even better now than upon my first reading decades ago.

There are bits and pieces on Italy. John was always fond of neighboring Italy; for years he lived just across the frontier in Haute-Savoie, itself once part of Italy, traveling up and down the country extensively, frequently on his motorbike. (One journey is beautifully re-created in *To the Wedding*.) In *White Bird*, John talks a lot about Italy, about Danilo Dolci's *Sicilian Lives*, about Italian painting and films like *Open City* and *Bicycle Thieves*, about having his rucksack stolen in Genoa from the back of his old Citroën 2CV car. There's also a lovely evocation of the poetry and life of the Roman poet Leopardi, one of Nietzsche's favorites, as well as a compelling essay on Van Gogh, called "The Production of the World." This one wasn't about Italy, of course; yet on my Italian Friday night, an essay I'd read many times seemed to speak to me like never before.

John would have been roughly my age (60ish) when he wrote about Van Gogh. He confesses to feeling washed out, at a low ebb, metaphysically exhausted. I was feeling washed out intellectually too, wondering what I'd do next, thinking I'd produced all I could, even talking about going into early retirement. I was still dizzy from my new life, living out a bit part in a Fellini movie, my very own *8 1/2*, thrilling though surreal, not feeling quite a whole number yet. I was suffering the same sense of unreality that John spoke about.

He'd hummed and hawed about going to a meeting in Amsterdam, he writes. In the end, he decided to go. And what transpires is a strange encounter with Van Gogh's paintings, with cornfields and potato eaters, pear trees and peasants dozing under giant haystacks, all of it kindling something inside him, unleashing a rebirth of sorts. "Within two minutes," he says, "and for the first time in three weeks—I was calm, reassured. Reality had been confirmed. The transformation was as quick and thoroughgoing as one of those sensational changes that can sometimes come about after an intravenous injection."

"These paintings," John says, "already very familiar to me, had never before manifested anything like this therapeutic power." And so, that night, sitting alone in a bar in Rome, John's words had never before manifested anything like this therapeutic power. Reading him was like being hooked up to an intravenous drip. Forget the wine. The transformation was immediate. Reality had been confirmed. I snapped out of it, I would get writing soon. I'd start that night; in fact, already had started that night, scribbling in my mental notebook, beginning to write *this*.

After I'd finished dinner and requested *il conto*, the young man behind the bar, who'd been serving me all night, asked what I'd been reading. I showed him *White Bird*, enunciating the author's name, an English writer and critic who died in 2017 at ninety, and who, I said, was widely available in Italian. "Never heard of him," he told me, almost apologetically. "That's a pity," I said, "because he's really something, a knockout read. You should check him out, his novels and criticism." I added that actually I'd written a book about him—a remark I immediately regretted, feeling like a drunken jerk, bragging about former glory days, like in the Springsteen song.

A week or so on, John was still with me, there in spirit. Or, better, I was still with him. When in Rome, I told myself . . . well, what better thing to do than to visit Gramsci, the great Italian Marxist, one of the founders of the Italian Communist Party (in 1921), whose grave lies in the city's "Non-Catholic Cemetery" in

Testaccio. Testaccio was a popular working-class neighborhood, housing thousands of industrial workers from nearby Ostiense, and probably best-known for Rome's famous slaughterhouse, at Mattatoio, in its heyday Europe's largest and most advanced. Decommissioned in 1975, it was partly renovated into an experimental cultural and arts center, with a farmers' market, but the huge complex remains mostly run-down, its old stockyards frequent hangouts for homeless populations.

The Non-Catholic Cemetery is just a short stroll away. Like Paris's Père Lachaise and London's Highgate, it's a grave-spotter's paradise. The English Romantic poet John Keats is its most popular denizen, followed by his famous champion, Percy Shelley. Gramsci, who occupies a secluded southwestern spot, is third on the visitors' roster. The day of my homage was searingly hot, over 40 degrees Celsius (104 Fahrenheit), and sitting on a wooden bench facing Gramsci, amid the din of cicadas, squawking birds, and mosquitos chomping at the bit, ancient cypress trees and pink flowers everywhere in bloom, I thought I'd landed on some distant tropical shore. The Aurelian city walls, towering over one side of the cemetery, made everything feel like a magic kingdom surrounded by a vast moat, cut off from the crazy chaos of the rest of the city; the 2,000-year-old Egyptian pyramid of Caius Cestius, its 36 meters poking out between the shrubbery, only added to the sense of otherworldliness.

Gramsci had a truly torrid life, rotting in fascist jails for a decade, yet his final resting place is lovely, serene in its elegance and simplicity. A small, upright stone slab reads:

GRAMSCI
ALES 1891 ROMA 1937

Its base is a marble casket, with a Latin inscription:

CINERA
ANTONII
GRAMSCII

Gramsci's ashes. Gramsci's sister-in-law, Tatiana Schucht, a Soviet citizen and sister of Giulia, the revolutionary's wife, was instrumental in securing him a plot at the cemetery. She'd been a student in Rome, living with her father, Apollo Schucht, who'd fled tsarist rule. Tatiana was devoted to her brother-in-law; and, in Giulia's absence (in the Soviet Union), cared for him during his confinement. In 1938, a year after his passing, with Mussolini's approval, she managed to get him a three-square-meter plot at the "English Cemetery."

In 1957, Gramsci's ashes were moved to another, larger plot, its current location, where I'm sitting now. At the back of Gramsci's headstone—I can see it if I bend my head round—is the name Apollo Schucht, Tatiana's father, inscribed as a memorial, as well as Nadine Schucht-Leontieva, her eldest sister, who'd died in 1919. Tatiana is the great unsung heroine in the Gramsci saga, her brother-in-law's political and emotional lifeline, not only burying him but keeping him alive, recovering all of his thirty-three notebooks, one of the most original and prodigious documents of modern Marxism.

Next to me that day, sharing the wooden bench, is a man in his mid-twenties, wearing AirPods, unperturbed about someone sitting so closely. We didn't say a word to each other; there seemed no point. For a while, I savor the setting, the peace, the moment, my Gramsci moment. Then one of the best essays written about Gramsci comes to mind: no surprise it's by John, the "open letter" he'd fired off to Subcomandante Marcos, the Zapatista

insurgent in Chiapas. John's letter, featured in his *The Shape of a Pocket* (2001), is a dispatch of great lyrical beauty, about "pockets of resistance," about hope and disobedience to the neoliberal world order; it's also about Sardinia and its stones, and about Gramsci, the island's radical patron saint.

"The least dogmatic of our century's thinkers about revolution," John writes to Marcos, "was Antonio Gramsci, no? His lack of dogmatism came from a kind of patience. This patience had absolutely nothing to do with indolence or complacency." "Gramsci believed in hope rather than promises," says John, "and hope is a long affair." Gramsci was born in the village of Ales and between age six and twelve went to school in the nearby town of Ghilarza, in central Sardinia. When he was four years old, as he was being carried, Antonio fell, crushed his back, and a spinal malformation ensued, as well as permanent ill health. (There's actually debate about whether this fall produced Gramsci's hunched back and stunted growth—he was less than five feet tall. In prison, Gramsci was diagnosed with suffering from longstanding Pott's disease, a form of tuberculosis of the spine that often creates back curvature and developmental problems.)

All around Ghilarza are stones, piles of stones, massive granite and limestone; others are smaller rocks gathered and stacked on the poor arid soil. Stones played a crucial role in Gramsci's life, John tells us. In Ghilarza, in a museum consecrated to his memory, a glass cabinet has a couple of local stones, about the size of grapefruits, which, every day, as a little boy, Gramsci lifted up and down to strengthen his weak shoulders and deformed back. Similar stones line the front of his grave now, perhaps not uncoincidentally chosen, placed there by well-wishers and followers in the know. I photograph some of them. They're also about the size of grapefruits. On a few, words are written, in assorted languages: "*Vous avez lutté. Nous luttons. Nous continuons à lutter*"

(You struggled. We struggle. We continue to struggle"). Some stones tack down handwritten notes: "*The old world is dying and the new world struggles to be born; now is the time of monsters.*"

It's a poetic rendering of a famous Gramsci passage, written in June 1930, in a translation often attributed to Slavoj Žižek. "The old world is dying," says Gramsci, in a more literal version, "and the new cannot be born; and in this interregnum a great variety of morbid symptoms appear." Gramsci meant a rift between past and future, between a present of great uncertainty, hobbled by morbidity, and a future stymied by monsters lurking around every corner; some, alas, hold office. Still, morbid politics doesn't reflect a monster's strength, Gramsci says, so much as it belies their weakness, is a condition of their fragility, a crisis of their authority.

Monsters aren't able to exert their hegemony no matter how many Capitols they storm or wars they manufacture. They bully and manipulate, for sure, might even dominate, but they're rarely leading or in control. What emerges, says Gramsci, is a "form of

politics that's cynical in its immediate manifestation." Meantime, he says, "the great masses have become detached from their traditional ideologies, no longer believing in what they used to believe previously." The "physical depression," Gramsci concludes, might "lead in the long run to a widespread skepticism, and a new 'arrangement' will be found."

In a letter to Tatiana, Gramsci says: "I don't like throwing stones in the dark; I like to have a concrete interlocutor or adversary." He was keen to stress the polemical nature of his prison writings, something that would enlarge his "inner life" in a tiny cell. We know they constituted a vast intellectual undertaking, begun in earnest in 1928 after the public prosecutor sentenced his brain to stop functioning for twenty years. Yet incarceration of a sickly body, besieged by uremia, hypertension, tubercular lesions, and gastroenteritis, could never restrain the brilliance of an active, inquisitive mind, a mind that could and had to "extract blood out of a stone" (as he also said of the political prisoner's plight).

One of this mind's desires was to overcome the divide between Marxism and everyday experience, between "a philosophy of praxis" and people's actual consciousness. "The popular element feels," says Gramsci, "but doesn't always know or understand." Demagogues prey on this slippage, stoke up people's raw feelings and visceral emotions, dislodge them from sound understanding, orchestrate "passive revolutions." On the other hand, "the intellectual element knows but doesn't always feel." Gramsci thinks these are "two extremes" that shouldn't necessarily be separate. By "popular element," he meant ordinary people who frequently intellectualize yet don't *function* as intellectuals. This isn't to prioritize one over the other so much as an appeal for knowledge and feeling to mutually interlock, to dialectically fuel each other.

What people feel largely stems from common sense, Gramsci says, from something immediate in their lives, from gossip and chatter, folklore and faith, vernacular and idiomatic language, from lotteries and tabloid newspapers, and social and mass media. Gramsci was a steely politico generous in his sympathy toward popular culture; ambivalent toward it, needless to say, because of its contradictoriness, because of its conservatism and reactionism. Yet common sense could likewise be "part critical and progressive," he says, something coherent with a "healthy nucleus."

The latter is the basis of Gramsci's "good sense," a common sense purged of stupidity and relieved of misconception. Good sense is what intellectuals—especially "organic intellectuals"— have to "renovate," somehow have to "make critical." To do so, Gramsci reckons, "the demands of cultural contact with the 'simple' must be continually felt." I can see John nodding in agreement, hear him saying, "*Yes, yes, yes.*" He certainly tried to keep this "organic cohesion" alive, the cultural contact with the simple continually felt throughout his long career of writing and activism. I remember him writing about other figures from Italian popular culture, too, about other artists and intellectuals likewise inspired by Gramsci, and by the cultural contact with the simple. One was filmmaker, poet, and essayist Pier Paolo Pasolini.

John quotes Pasolini in an essay he wrote in 2006 about Pasolini's 1963 film *La Rabbia* (*Rage*): "For we never have despair without some small hope." Pasolini also loved Gramsci, even created an affecting poem about him, "The Ashes of Gramsci" (1954), reciting it beside the Sardinian's tomb (in its old location). It took one to know one: a poem written by a man assassinated by fascists about a man assassinated by fascists:

Here you lie, exiled, with cruel Protestant
neatness, listed among the foreign
dead: Gramsci's ashes . . . Between hope
and my ancient distrust, I draw near you, happening by chance
on this meagre greenhouse, in the presence of your grave, in the
presence of your spirit, afoot, down here among the free
And, of this country which would not let you rest,
I feel this an injustice: your mental strain
—here among the silences of the dead—what reason
    our troubled destiny
Will you ask of me, dead man, unadorned,
that I abandon this hopeless
passion to be in the world?

John watched Pasolini's film more than forty years after its making. It had never been publicly shown in Pasolini's lifetime. In 1962, Italian TV had an idea to ask Pasolini to make a documentary about why everywhere in the world there was fear of war. He made the film, but when the television companies saw it, they balked, got cold feet. John thinks *La Rabbia* "is a film inspired by a fierce sense of endurance, not anger. Pasolini looks at what is happening with unflinching lucidity." And his answer to the original question was simple: "The class struggle explains war."

John says two anonymous voices are spoken in the film, two of Pasolini's friends, one of whom was likewise John's friend, the painter Renato Guttuso, whose artwork was chosen to adorn the first postwar membership card of the Italian Communist Party (PCI). Guttuso drew particular inspiration for his neorealist paintings from two sources: Picasso's *Guernica* and Gramsci's *Prison Notebooks*.

A little while after my cemetery visit, I had another experience with John in Rome, an uncanny one, this time also encountering Renato Guttuso. I was in a branch of the large bookstore chain Feltrinelli, perusing the art section, looking at images rather than texts in a language I could still barely understand—when, all of a sudden, right in front of me, almost beckoning me, finding me rather than I finding it, was John's book on Renato Guttuso. It had been freshly put into Italian by a small Palermo press, under the stewardship of journalist, essayist, editor, and translator Maria Nadotti. Maria has been a dedicated champion of John over the years and through her books and translations made his work accessible to Italian audiences. In 2019, she produced a wonderfully quirky collection about John's passion for motor-bikes, *Sulla motocicletta*, with a translated piece from yours truly on "Spinoza's Motorcycle," my riff on John's riff on the Dutch philosopher from *Bento's Sketchbook*.

Maria's latest translation, like *Sulla motocicletta*, is a lovely little work of art in its own right, produced by an independent press that appears less concerned with bottom-line dictates than with creating an object of intense beauty, a labor of love with artisanal integrity, never intending it to be anything com-mercial. A few years ago, I'd sent Maria an email, congratulat-ing her on *Sulla motocicletta*, receiving a response: "I miss John enormously," she said. "The only way I find to compensate for his physical absence is to work on his texts, words, ideas, and to keep 'conspiring.'" And so here was Maria again conspiring with John, resuscitating a book over half-a-century old, with a publisher based in Guttuso's native Sicily.

What's fascinating about *Guttuso* is that it was in fact John's first book, from 1957. And yet, oddly, it was a ninety-page text written in English that never appeared in English, going straight into German under the auspices of Dresden's Verlag der Kunst, edited by John's friend Erhard Frommhold. (John said he was

always indebted to Frommhold; it was he who'd given John
the belief that he could become not only a writer but a writer of
books.) Maria had somehow managed to unearth John's original dog-eared typescript from his British Library archives, with
handwritten annotations and missing pages, and set herself the
task of reconstructing it, of re-creating it in Italian. How thrilled
John would have been had he seen it!

At one point in her introduction, Maria discusses the link
between John and Elizabeth David's *Italian Food*, a book
of *Guttuso*'s generation, and how Guttuso had been commissioned to do its illustrations. Apparently John had a copy
of *Italian Food* when he lived in London, cooking from it often
at his flat at 4 Nutley Ter in South Hampstead, without ever
realizing that inside was Guttuso's artwork. One of the book's
most arresting images is of a lone workman, dressed in simple
jacket and striped shirt, eating a pasta lunch, literally shoveling
it into his mouth ravenously; a tumbler of red wine lies beside
him. Guttuso captures the intense, quasi-religious devotion of a

man to an everyday meal, savoring it as if it were his last supper. Elizabeth David quickly realized that "the dangerously blazing vitality" Guttuso invested in the commissioned artwork became "an integral part of my book."

In a photo of a wistful-looking Guttuso, taken in 1956 in his Rome studio at Villa Massimo, a similar image of the pasta-lunching laborer can be seen tacked to the wall alongside a poster of Picasso's *Guernica* and a couple of tatty photographs of Antonio Gramsci. Picasso and Gramsci were Guttuso's cult heroes. John points out Guttuso's "inherent connection between art and politics: politics being used in the broadest sense of the word to describe that struggle of social forces which underlies any particular social order." "Guttuso reacted strongly against the neo-classicism being encouraged by the fascists," John says. On the other flank, his adherence to the Communist Party *and* to avant-garde modernist art, to so-called *picassismo*, also meant a sometimes fraught relationship to the Party, with its espousal of Socialist Realism, mimicking Gramsci's own fraught relationship to the party he'd helped found. The pair's "cultural politics" was mistrusted by those who saw Marxism as the iron laws of economism.

When Gramsci died, Guttuso would have been a young man of twenty-six. We can assume they never met. But Guttuso would have absolutely encountered firsthand Gramsci's onetime friend and co-founder of *Ordine Nuovo* newspaper, Palmiro Togliatti, the PCI's Secretary, formerly Gramsci's closest political ally and fellow Party brainchild. (Togliatti and Gramsci fell out not long after the former took the PCI's helm in 1927, each taking opposing stances toward Stalin's Marxist-Leninist orthodoxy.) John points out that Guttuso's own commitment to the Party and to the working classes was no less resolute because of his expressionist art. "It is the everyday life of Italy," he writes, "the carrying

in of the weight of the harvest, the determination of the miner, the setting up of the telegraph poles throughout the landscape, the terracing of the hills, that Guttuso celebrates."

Maybe this reflects what John says defines Guttuso's art: that "it is outstanding because it so obviously implies an ambitious and compelling sense of *obligation*" (emphasis added). "One can only grow through obligations," repeats John, in a phrase he attributes to Antoine Saint-Exupéry. *Obligation* is the operative word, a sense of service and commitment, duty-bound, an acknowledgment of a necessary interaction between art and life. John goes to pains to underscore this notion of obligation, and I wonder now, after drafting these words, after working through my own thoughts about John, kickstarted by my re-reading of *White Bird*—whether that night at the bar in Monti, whether it was obligation I felt, an obligation to keep John's spirit alive, to continue to struggle artistically and creatively as he had struggled, to "conspire" with him as Maria Nadotti had said, and to continue to keep the Red Flag flying; to be obligated to Gramsci, too, a sentiment reinforced by those stones I'd seen at his graveside, stones about the size of the grapefruits he'd exercised with as a small boy.

So a strange sense of obligation had come over me at the cemetery as well, compelling me to return there, where I spoke to Tatiana, a good omen maybe, the coordinator of the Visitor's Center. She'd told me that they were always looking for responsible volunteers to work here, young as well as older people. The cemetery is a private institution, she said, receives no public funding, and survives exclusively on donations and volunteer services. And it is still active, welcoming visitors at the same time as it respects families of the deceased, holding funerals and burials, tending gravestones, ensuring the general upkeep of a magnificent verdant landscape.

In my book *Marx, Dead and Alive*, I wrote about Marx in London's Highgate Cemetery, shocked at the desecration of his tomb by vandals; they'd daubed it with red paint and walloped it with a lump hammer. I'd been attracted by the specialness of Highgate, by its peacefulness and tranquility, and was dismayed at the demented violence shown toward it and Marx. I guess I felt something similar here in Rome, felt an allure and fascination, and maybe, in these right-shifting political times, also had a similar concern for Gramsci's fate, that he was safe, because I decided, there and then, to offer my services as a volunteer at the cemetery if they wanted me.

A few days on, I met Yvonne, the cemetery's director, an American who's lived in Italy for twenty-five years and has a PhD in Art History. She wondered why I wanted to volunteer. I said I had time and wanted to be near Gramsci. Yvonne feels strongly about the contemplative atmosphere of the cemetery, about its slow, "unplugged" ambience. Visitors need to be sensitive, she said, that the cemetery is a site of peace, reflection, and remembrance, not another tourist spectacle for Instagram selfies or posting comic videos. She wants to nudge visitors off their cameras and iPhones, get them into "live" experience.

After my interview, Yvonne welcomed me to the cemetery, happy to have me on board, but suggested I continue to learn Italian. Then she admitted that she had used Gramsci in her own studies on the conservation of historic sites in Orte, a town fifty miles north of Rome. Gramsci, she said, was for her the cemetery's most important person, its special VIP. As I exited, excited about my new part-time role, walking up Via Caio Cestio back into the bustle of the city again, I thought to myself that henceforth I'm not only going to try to keep Gramsci's spirit alive—now, incredibly, I'm also going to keep an eye on him dead.

Coda: Maria Nadotti and John visited Rome's Non-Catholic Cemetery together on October 12, 2014. "John sat a long while beside the grave of Gramsci," Maria told me, "then drew a stone in a sketchbook. Finally, he put the drawing on the grave among the other stones."

Maria took three photographs of John Berger. "It was a very intense private moment," she said, "but I believe that John would be happy to share it and make it public."

I am very grateful to her for letting me use these images.

2

A ROSE

I'm standing under the entrance arch of the Hotel Villa Morgagni along Via Giovanni Battista Morgagni, in Rome's northeastern Nomentano neighborhood. Morgagni is a smart-looking mansion-cum-townhouse, built in a turn-of-the-century Liberty style, with fetching Art Nouveau flourishes. Since the early 2000s, the property has been owned by the Italian businessman Adartico Vudafieri, a former rally car champion, who transformed it into a 4-star, 34-room, luxury boutique hotel, equipped with Jacuzzis and conference room facilities.

Ninety-seven years back, Via Giovanni Battista Morgagni, number 25, was a more modest lodging house, home of a quietly discreet *pensionante* called Antonio Gramsci. It was here, around 10:30 PM on November 8, 1926, that Mussolini's fascist henchmen, who'd been surveying Gramsci's every move in the months prior, raided his room, confiscated his documents, and arrested him as an "enemy of the state." (It wasn't the first time his room had been ransacked.) He was carted off to Rome's Regina Coeli penitentiary and immediately placed in solitary confinement. A small plaque on the hotel's gatepost, with a poignant inscription, commemorates Gramsci's sojourn at Morgagni, memorializing him as a rare "leader who knew how to listen":

Gramsci's landlady, Clara Passarge, a Prussian-born woman, was particularly disgruntled by those evening's dramatic events, taking it very badly. Gramsci was her and husband Giorgio's favorite tenant—the "professor" they affectionately called him, on account of his bookish nature, a scholarly-looking little man forever transporting caseloads of texts and papers to and from his rented room. (The professorial assumption wouldn't have been unreasonable: Sapienza University of Rome was, after all, only a block away down the road from his dwelling.) Gramsci, of course, was no university academic. Journalist, Italian Communist Party's (PCI) general secretary, he'd already been elected to Italy's Chamber of Deputies, a position that should have given him immunity from such a politically motivated arrest. But Mussolini had schemed up Special Laws of Defense, rendering illegal any form of anti-fascist activity, depriving Gramsci and hundreds of other progressive deputies of their parliamentary mandate.

For a customarily cautious man, whose careful analysis had seen fascist forces brewing, it was a mystery why Gramsci had left himself so open to arrest. He knew he was being followed, watched everywhere and at all hours; he'd felt "the storm coming," he told sister-in-law Tatiana ("Tania"), "in an indistinct and instinctive way." Meanwhile, fearing for the safety of pregnant wife, Giulia, and infant son Delio, he insisted they return to Moscow, where Gramsci's second son, Giuliano, who would never see his father, was born on August 30, 1926.

In a way, Gramsci seemed more bothered about the "trouble and inconveniences" he'd caused the Passarges the night of his arrest. The first of his famous *Letters from Prison*, written in the Regina Coeli penitentiary (undated), addressed to his landlady, is a touching expression of regret: "Dearest Signora, first of all, I want to apologize for the trouble and inconveniences I have caused you, which in truth formed no part of our tenancy agreement." Gramsci asks her to forward onto him a few of his books, including his beloved *Divine Comedy*, and "prepare some of my underclothes and hand them over to a good woman called Marietta Bucciarelli, when she comes on my behalf." He adds, "If my stay in this place should last long, I think you should consider the room free and do as you wish with it. You can pack the books and throw away the newspapers. I apologize again, dear Signora, and offer my regrets which are as deep as your kindness is great.

My regards to Signor Giorgio and to the young lady [Clara's daughter]; with heartfelt respect, Antonio Gramsci." The letter is all the more touching because it never reached its destination.

A few weeks on, Gramsci again wrote his landlady (November 30, 1926), telling her he'd been three days in a Palermo jail: "I left Rome on the morning of the twenty-fifth for Naples, where I stayed for a few days and was devoured by insects. In a few days, I will leave for the island of Ustica, to which I have been assigned for my *confino*. During my journey, I was unable to send back the keys to the house: as soon as I arrive at Ustica I will forward them immediately and I'll send you the precise address and instructions for sending me or having sent to me the things that I'll be able to keep here and that may be useful to me. My health is fairly good; I'm a bit tired, that's all. Inform Maria if she comes to see you and ask her to give my regards to all my relatives and friends who still remember me. Kind regards to Signor Giorgio and to the Signorina; cordially, A. Gramsci." Again, the letter never found its destination, again confiscated by Mussolini's political police. (Both letters, incidentally, never saw the public light of day until the early 1970s.)

As it happened, Signora Clara didn't last long after Gramsci's arrest; likely he'd suspected all wasn't well. He'd asked Tatiana (March 19, 1927), "How is my landlady, or did she die?" He confessed, "I'm afraid the scene of my arrest may have helped accelerate her illness, because she liked me very much and looked so pale when they took me away." Gramsci said he'd received a letter from Giorgio Passarge in early January 1927, "who was desperate and thought that his wife's death was immanent, then I no longer heard anything. Poor woman." Signora Passarge would pass away on February 19, 1927, aged sixty-five.

Not long after my visit to Gramsci's old lodgings and site of arrest, I discovered something I'd hitherto not known: Clara

Passarge is likewise a denizen of Rome's Non-Catholic Cemetery. I'd spotted her gravestone, looking rather forlorn and untended, on one of my regular inspections of the tombs and their environs. Seeing Gramsci and his former landlady reunited, sharing the same abode again, struck me as a strange quirk of fate, just as my witnessing it strikes me as a strange quirk of fate, finding myself before both of them now, a volunteer at the cemetery.

Clara's grave prompted me to look her up in the cemetery's death register, where I managed to track down the original hand-written entry. Then I did the same for Gramsci, wondering why I hadn't done so before; sure enough, he's there, too, registered in the same hand a little more than a decade after the Signora's passing.

To say that Clara's grave looked forlorn and untended isn't exactly the whole truth. For there's another story to her being at

the cemetery, another connection involving an impressive, far from forlorn, white marble sculpture located just behind Clara's tombstone, tucked into an alcove of the Aurelian wall. It's a striking, haunting, structure known as *The Bride*, a life-size (and life-like) reclining young woman, on her deathbed. A rose is sometimes placed in her hand, a gesture said to bring good luck to the giver. The bride in question is Elsbeth Wegener Passarge, none other than Clara Passarge's eldest daughter, who died in 1902, tragically of typhus, at the age of eighteen. She was born in Prussia to Clara's first husband (Giorgio was Elsbeth's stepfather), yet grew up in Rome, later engaged to be married to an Austrian sculptor, Ferdinand Seeboeck. The couple were deeply in love. But the husband-and-wife pairing wasn't meant to be, and as a memorial to his late fiancée, Ferdinand created *The Bride*, with, on its base, written in Italian and German, the following words: "*She passes from a sweet dream of love to the life of angels*." It took Ferdinand thirty years to get his sculpture installed in its current site, during which time he relinquished his own plot beside his bride, in favor of her mother, Clara, whose remains now lie beside her daughter's, and not in the marked grave nearby.

THE DAY I DISCOVERED CLARA'S TOMBSTONE, GRAMSCI'S marble casket was adorned with a beautiful red rose. At that moment, sitting close by on what I now like to call "Gramsci's bench," was an elderly gent, in his mid-seventies, portly, with long, flowing gray hair, clad in scruffy shorts and a stained white undervest. Beside him, a shopping bag full of old clothes. Maybe he was homeless or semi-destitute? He looked content next to Gramsci, and, as I passed, taking a photo of the red rose on the casket, I engaged him in conversation. He was an old communist,

he said, and Gramsci his hero. He comes here often, to pay his respects. Was it he, I wondered, who'd left that red rose?

For a while, we spoke about Giorgio Napolitano, a former high-ranking PCI leader, modern Italy's longest standing president, who died in late September, age ninety-eight, and who was about to be laid to rest in the Non-Catholic Cemetery. The man in the white vest said Gramsci was better known abroad than in Italy; I was inclined to concur, but knew too that plenty of Italians, many young Italians included, visit the cemetery to see Gramsci, and talk about him as if he were still alive and kicking. Then the man in the white vest mentioned Benedetto Croce and Giovanni Gentile, two of Gramsci's interlocutors and antagonists. I said, as a by-the-way comment, that Antonio Labriola, an older generation Italian Marxist, another early influence from Gramsci's Turin student days, and frequently referenced in *The Prison Notebooks*, is buried not far away, in an impressive, opulent grave in the *Zona Prima*. The man in the white vest seemed to want to talk more about Gentile and Croce and about Gramsci's views on education.

Croce was a liberal, Gentile a fascist. Both started out as vaguely *marxisant* Hegelian philosophers before the former drifted toward the center and the latter toward the far right. Each wrote about education; in the early 1920s, Gentile became Mussolini's Minister of Education. But Gramsci rejected, on the one side, Croce's liberal reductionism, which saw civil society as the realm of free individuality, somehow apart from the state, and, on the other, Gentile's statist reductionism, where civil society got devoured entirely by the state. Gramsci's line is more subtle. He never makes any "organic" distinction between state and civil society. The separation, he said, is analytical and methodological; state and civil society are conjoined, dialectically intertwined, operative together, yet theoretically distinguishable.

From prison, Gramsci cast a keen critical eye on the so-called Gentile Reform Act of 1923, where, among other things, religious education had become compulsory in elementary schools. *Letters from Prison* frequently ask Tatiana for copies of Gentile's texts and speeches, a lot featured in a rather ominous sounding *Educazione Fascista*. Gentile's educational reform also introduced an entrance exam for acceptance into middle school, which, says Gramsci, privileged upper-class kids, relegating their working-class and peasant counterparts to technical and training schools.

Gramsci was a bit old school in his educational beliefs. He says Gentile's education act failed to provide the specific teaching of Italian grammar, thereby excluding "the national-popular masses from learning language, confining them to the ghetto of dialect." (Gramsci advocated the teaching of Latin, for instance, because it "combines and satisfies a whole series of pedagogic and psychological requirements.") "Active" schools, he says, aren't elitist institutions nor sites of rote and factual inculcation. Yet neither should they encourage liberal laissez-faire free-play and voluntarist free-will, where individualities are seen as beyond any conditioning social relations and social institutions. Gramsci calls for a "nexus between instruction and education," a curriculum that teaches critical, socially aware thinking at the same time as it develops students' creative capacities, accustoming them to reason, to think abstractly and schematically, while "remaining able to plunge back from abstraction into real and immediate life."

For Gramsci, self-discipline and self-control are vital in learning. Students need to condition themselves to long hours of concentration, he says, to sitting still, developing bodily endurance as well as a lively mind, training their muscles and nerves as well as their brains. Learning can be tough, he says, an ethos likely gleaned from his own history as a lowly youth and studious prison inmate. It isn't only manual labor that requires sweat and toil. Indeed, if ever the working classes were to develop their own brand of hardy and smart "organic intellectuals," with the appropriate attributes and skills to help transform society, they'll need, Gramsci thinks, an educational system very different from the one Gentile is proposing.

THE MAN IN THE WHITE VEST AND I SHAKE HANDS AND bid each other *arrivederci*. Wandering back to my duties at the cemetery's Visitor's Center, leaving him with Gramsci and that red rose, I realized I'd forgotten to ask if it was he who had laid the flower there. I never got the chance to talk with him, either, about the significance of roses for Gramsci and how growing them became almost as much a passion as filling his thirty-three scholastic notebooks.

After Gramsci was transferred in July 1928 to the Turi prison for the infirm and disabled in Bari, Calabria, he began, in a little plot of soil along a sidewall of its courtyard, to grow different plants and flowers. His letters to Tatiana and Giulia thereafter fill up with news of their progress. On April 22, 1929, he wrote Tatiana: "On one fourth of a square meter I want to plant four or five seeds of each kind and see how they turn out." He asks his sister-in-law if she can get hold of sweet pea, spinach, carrot, chicory, and celery seeds.

Gramsci says he's become more patient, "but only by virtue of a great effort to control myself." He seems to take inspiration from his flowers and plants, from their slow and persistent growth, from the rose he's trying to cultivate, patiently and persistently—against all odds. "The rose has fallen victim of a dreadful sunstroke," he says, "all the leaves in the more tender parts are burnt and carbonized; it has a desolate, sad aspect, but it is putting out new buds." Seemingly referring to himself, he adds: "It isn't dead, at least not yet." In Gramsci's letters, the plight of his dear rose strikes as an allegory of his own dear plight.

"The seeds have been very slow in pushing up small sprouts," he tells Tatiana, again maybe referring to himself and to the life of a Marxist radical; "an entire series obstinately insists on living an underground life." Each day, Gramsci says, he's seized by the temptation to pull at them a little, making them grow a little faster. "I remain undecided," he admits, "between two concepts of the world and of education: whether to follow Rousseau and leave things to nature, which is never wrong and is basically good, or to be a voluntarist and force nature, introducing into the evolution the expert hand of humanity and the principle of authority. Until now the uncertainty persists and the two ideologies joust in my head."

Still, Gramsci's voluntarist environmentalism—the intervention of human authority and action—doesn't impose itself brutally on nature. He lovingly cares for his rose, admires its beauty and tenderness, the delicate texturing of its petals, its poetic quality, the radiance of its blossoming, often sounding the way Saint-Exupéry's Petit Prince would sound a decade on, nurturing his own rose; at the same time, Gramsci marvels at how robust his rose is, how hardy, struggling to survive, persisting on living, sometimes on the point of death, yet pulling through with new buds despite the impending "solar catastrophe."

Elsewhere, Gramsci says to Tatiana: "The rose is beginning to bud after it had seemed reduced to desolate twigs. But will it manage to survive the approaching summer heat? It looks puny and run-down to be up to the task. It is true of course that, at bottom, the rose is nothing but a wild thorn bush, and therefore very vital." Again, maybe with himself in mind, we might recall one revealing letter he'd written Tatiana, earlier in his incarceration

(February 19, 1927), taking the boat with other prisoners to Ustica. One of the banished was an "anarchist type," Gramsci says, called "Unico," a sort of superintendent, who upon hearing Gramsci introduce himself to other inmates, "stared at me for a long time, then he asked: 'Gramsci, Antonio?' 'Yes, Antonio!' I answered. 'That can't be,' he retorted, 'because Antonio Gramsci must be a giant and not a little squirt like you.'"

On February 10, 1930, Gramsci writes Tatiana: "So, then, become more energetic; cure your will too, do not let the southern winds fill you with languor. The bulbs have sprouted already, indeed some time back; one of the hyacinths already shows the colors of its future flower. Provided the frost doesn't destroy everything. The rose has also borne new buds; it is wilder than ever, it seems a thorn bush instead of a rose, but the vegetal vigor of the thorn bush is also interesting. I embrace you affectionately, Antonio."

TODAY, OCTOBER 17, 2023, GRAMSCI'S GRAVE IS COVERED with brilliant flowers, blooming everywhere, a sight to behold. Who could have placed them all here? Today as well I began to think about what it was I wanted to stress in this book. If earlier I spoke of stones and a sense of obligation—obligation to Gramsci, to Marxist politics, to the left, a sentiment somehow reinforced by the grapefruit-size rocks a deformed Gramsci lifted as a child—now, I think it's the rose I want to emphasize, a rose for Gramsci, and the notion of *resilience*. Not just of our intervening to nurture nature, to sustain ourselves ecologically, but of an individual capacity for resilience, a stoicism to resist, to learn and educate oneself, to promulgate a politics of emancipation even in incarceration, even in an inferno resembling Dante's.

"It seems to me that under such conditions prolonged for years," Gramsci told his younger brother Carlo (December 19,

1929), "and with such psychological experience, a person should have reached the loftiest stage of stoic serenity and should have acquired such a profound conviction that humans bear within themselves the source of their own moral strength, that everything depends on them, on their energy, on their will, on the iron coherence of the aims they set for themselves and the means they adopt to realize them, that they will never again despair and lapse into those vulgar, banal states of mind that are called pessimism and optimism. My state of mind synthesizes these two emotions and overcomes them: I'm a pessimist because of intelligence, but an optimist because of will."

Today, these Gramsci flowers remind me of Elsa Morante's epic novel called *History*, on the horrors of Nazism/fascism, and the rape of a young woman by an adolescent German soldier (killed a few days later on the front) and her fierce battle to raise her bastard child in the horror of it all, in a world Gramsci often said was "great and terrible," and her hope that hope would win out in the end. Her final words, borrowing from a Gramsci letter,

never mention him by name, only his Turi prison number:7047:
"All the seeds have failed except one; I don't know what it is, but
probably it is a flower and not a weed." That's it, that's what I
want to say: flowers will always outlast weeds.

3

ANIMALITY

The Non-Catholic Cemetery isn't just the home of the dead with buried tales: it's also full of tails, of stray cats, a living colony of twenty-five or so semi-feral moggies. We know from old paintings of the nearby Pyramid, especially those by the Roman artist Bartolomeo Pinelli, that cats have freely roamed the area for over a hundred and fifty years. Nowadays, tourists and locals alike come to see the cemetery's *gatti*, longtime beneficiaries of well-wisher donations and skilled volunteer caregivers, cat women who regularly nourish and tend the cat colony's veterinarian needs. The most famous of the cemetery's felines is the late "Romeo," a three-legged tabby who passed away in 2006, laid to rest in his own mini-tomb not far from Gramsci's.

Many cats have their favorite spots where they're often seen sniffing the scent of late departed ones, their bones and ashes. Gramsci, too, has a familiar prowler and protector, a big white and gray with an apparent penchant for revolutionary communism. He's always wandering about the PCI founder's tomb, oftentimes lying across his casket, or else upright on it, head aloft, proudly standing to attention, on the lookout for reactionary trouble—a mini-militia of one keeping a left paw out for old Gramsci. Perhaps we might label this loyal moggie "The General," after Engels's old sobriquet, and our General knows intuitively, like most animals, where his bread is buttered—who is friend or foe. Gramsci, of course, was a dear friend, an animal lover whose humanist life and thought forever embraced non-human comradery.

Prison Notebooks sets the tone with "Animality and Industrialism," Gramsci's original work-in-progress header for the section

he'd eventually label "Americanism and Fordism." No metaphor intended. The history of industrialism, Gramsci says, "has always been a continuing struggle against the element of 'animality' in man." "It has been an interrupted, often painful and bloody process," he says, "of subjugating natural (i.e. animal and primitive) instincts to new, more complex and rigid norms and habits of order, exactitude, and precision which are a necessary consequence of industrial development." Animality, we might say, is a more instinctive life spirit, something looser, more rambunctious and libertine, potentially more subversive, unsettling for the soberer necessities of workforce obediency. As Gramsci puts it, "The exaltation of passion cannot be reconciled with the timed movements of productive motions connected with the most perfected automatism."

That's why the bourgeoisie must constantly wage war against animality, why its "puritanical struggles" get embedded in the state. Gramsci reckons it's another historical instance of how "changes in the modes of existence and modes of life have taken place through brute coercion, that is to say through the domination of one group over all the productive forces of society." New forms of productive organization beget new kinds of "education," new forms of coercion and consent to condition people to industry's developmental needs. Henry Ford was a classic pioneer, patrolling not only how his workforce labored on the assembly line—deploying F. W. Taylor's "scientific management" techniques—but also how workers led their private lives, monitoring how they spent their wages, advocating a "morality" more appropriate for the "true" America—at least for a certain stratum of its populace.

With his infamous phrase "trained gorilla," Taylor threw back in the faces of workers the whole idea of animality. Gramsci calls it "brutally cynical." Yet, in truth, he also knew that such repetitive, soul-sapping activity—indeed any kind of grinding, contentless work in whatever division of labor—blue-collar, white-collar, no collar or otherwise—is a venture no gorilla would ever likely deign to undertake. "I prefer not to," they'd probably say, if they could talk human language. Or else they'd become, as John Berger said in his well-known essay "Why Look at Animals?" (1977), like an animal in a zoo, "lethargic and dull. (As frequent as the calls of animals in a zoo are the cries of children demanding: Where is he? Why doesn't he move? Is he dead?)." Berger also reminds us how most modern techniques of social conditioning were first established with animal experiments.

Gramsci defends animality against the "moral order" of social conditioning—in both its capitalist and communist guises. In *Prison Notebooks*, he expressed disagreement with a certain "Leone Davidovi," a.k.a. Leon Trotsky, who'd been *pro* the rationalization and militarization of work under Soviet Communism. "Every worker feels himself a soldier of labor," Trotsky said, "who cannot dispose of himself freely; if the order is given . . . he must carry it out; if he does not carry it out, he will be a deserter who is punished." Gramsci says this military model was "a pernicious prejudice and the militarization of labor a failure." The fact that workers no longer have to think about their work and get no immediate satisfaction from carrying out its repetitive tasks means, Gramsci says, that they have opportunities to think about other things, perhaps even leading to "a train of thought that is far from conformist."

Eight months before the October Revolution, a youthful Gramsci had already mulled over how bourgeois discipline ought to differ from socialist discipline—how the former's mechanical and authoritarian paradigms are at variance with socialist paradigms. Bourgeois discipline, he wrote in *La città futura*, "keeps the bourgeois aggregation firmly together. Discipline must be met with discipline." Everybody obeys in the bourgeois state. Its model, Gramsci says, is English colonialism in India, ironized in Rudyard Kipling's short story "Her Majesty's Servants" (from *The Jungle Book*): horses obey the soldiers riding them, soldiers obey sergeants, sergeants obey lieutenants, lieutenants captains, captains majors, majors colonels, colonels brigadiers, brigadiers generals, and generals the Viceroy who in turn obeys the Queen. Everybody moves in unison, has their role strictly defined, drilled into them, each and all obeying one another in a tight, rigid hierarchy, extendedly reproduced. "Thus it is done," says Kipling, "because you cannot do otherwise, you are our subjects."

Socialist discipline, by contrast, "is autonomous and spontaneous," says Gramsci. "Whoever is a socialist or wants to become one does not obey; they command themselves; they impose a rule of life on their impulses, on their disorderly aspirations." The discipline imposed on citizens by the bourgeois state turns them into subjects. Socialist discipline is counterwise, turning subjects into citizens, "a citizen who is now rebellious, precisely because they have become conscious of their personality and feel it is shackled and cannot freely express itself in the world." Maybe this is what Gramsci meant by animality: something unshackled, not caged in a zoo. "I want to plunge into animality," he'd said in 1916, "to draw from it new vigor."

IN A LETTER TO DELIO FROM 1936, GRAMSCI IS A LITTLE stern, warning his young son of the dangers of "anthropomorphism," of attributing human traits to animals. In this case, Delio refers his father to elephants. Delio had had the bright idea that elephants might one day evolve and walk on two legs, becoming, like humans, capable of conquering the forces of nature. Yet Papa reverses the anthropomorphic hypothesis of Delio's, querying, "Why should the elephant have evolved like man? Who knows whether some wise old elephant or some whimsical young little elephant doesn't from his point of view think up hypotheses as to why man has not become a proboscidiform creature." Then, a few sentences on, maybe wary that he's getting heavy with his son, Gramsci softens his tone, and through animals tries to kindle his son's vivid imagination rather than dampen it: "In the court-yard," he tells Delio, "I always see two pairs of blackbirds and the cats who crouch in ambush, ready to pounce; but it doesn't seem that the blackbirds worry about it and their flitting about is always gay and elegant. I embrace you. Papa."

Animals help Gramsci connect with his long-lost son. Giuliano is too young to really write to his father, so Dad's focus is on Delio, often desperately attempting to embrace a child he was conscious of losing touch of—going to school, reading books, growing up, becoming Russian, speaking Russian—all of it slip-ping away from Gramsci's grasp; his letters reveal the frustration and desperation of a father who wanted to know, who tried to cling on. "In truth," he told wife Giulia (letter dated December 14, 1931), "I'm unable psychologically to establish a rapport with them because concretely I know nothing about their life and their development."

He tries very hard in many letters, oftentimes too hard, talking to a child as if he were an adult, only underscoring the growing distance—the emotional, temporal, and spatial distance—from him and his family. Gramsci didn't always know it, but Giulia herself was frequently absent from childrearing, institutionalized with periodic mental breakdowns and bouts of depression, leav-ing Gramsci's sons in the care of his other sister-in-law, Eugenia. Once close, over the years mutual resentment grew between Eugenia and her brother-in-law Antonio.

"When I was a boy," Gramsci again writes Delio (February 22, 1932), "I raised many birds as well as other animals: falcons, barn owls, cuckoos, magpies, crows, goldfinches, canaries, chaffinches, larks, etc. I raised a small snake, a weasel, a hedgehog, and some turtles ... I amused myself by bringing live snakes into the courtyard to see how the hedgehog would hunt them." Little wonder, then, does Gramsci recommend to his son Kipling's story about Rikki-Tikki-Tavi, the intrepid snake-sleighing mongoose from *The Jungle Book*. Rikki-Tikki-Tavi is one of Kipling's most endearing (and enduring) characters, a featherweight who takes out heavyweights, huge cobras and black mambas. His "business in life," Kipling says, "was to fight and eat snakes." A little underdog—or undergoose—who tackles bigger, more powerful foes, brandishing agility and cunning. Perhaps it's not too difficult to see why Gramsci might be so charmed by the tale.

Kipling, peculiarly, appears as one of Gramsci's favorite authors. The English novelist, short story writer, poet, and journalist crops up often in Gramsci's works—in his letters, *Prison Notebooks*, and cultural essays—sometimes in surprising contexts, reappropriated in unexpected, imaginative ways. In prison, Gramsci even translated Kipling's most famous poem "If—," published in 1910, once Britain's best loved verse. Although Kipling won the Nobel Prize for Literature in 1907, when Gramsci read

him he was scarcely known in Italy. Thus it's not entirely clear how Gramsci got wind of the colonial scribe, all the more given his right-leaning, anti-communist politics, and racist language— notwithstanding an enormous sensitivity to teeming, poor Indian street life. (Kipling did make the Italian news in May 1917, when, at the behest of the *Daily Telegraph,* he visited the Italian front to write a series of firsthand dispatches, later published in pamphlet form as *The War in the Mountains: Impressions from the Italian Front.* Gramsci would have likely known about such a trip and read Kipling's five articles in Risorgimento Press's Italian paper- back edition.)

In *Quaderno No.3,* Gramsci makes a comment on Kipling that reads like a note to self: "Could Kipling's work serve to criticize a certain society that claims to be something without developing the corresponding civic morality within itself, indeed having a mode of being contradictory with the goals that it verbally sets itself?" "Kipling's morality is imperialistic," Gramsci says, "only when it is closely linked to a very specific historical reality: but images of powerful immediacy can be extracted from it for every social group that fights for political power."

We know from Gramsci's letters that he'd read Kipling in French. (Kipling himself was an ardent Francophile.) Ironically, Kipling's poetry was admired by interwar Soviet avant-garde writers, so one might surmise that Gramsci picked up on Kipling through those channels; but that doesn't quite stack up because Gramsci had already referenced *The Jungle Book* well before the Bolsheviks had seized power. In fact, Gramsci sometimes signed off his *Avanti!* and *Il Grido del Popolo* (The Cry of the People) articles with the pseudonym "Raksha," after the formidable she- wolf protector of Mowgli, *The Jungle Book's* "man-cub," whom Raksha adopts as part of her wolf family, fending off the noto- rious tiger Shere Khan who tries to eat baby Mowgli. Raksha becomes a kind of animal organic intellectual, clearly inspirational for Gramsci.

Meanwhile, Kipling's darker tales, like "The Strange Ride of Morrowbie Jukes" (1885), spoke to Gramsci on a gut level. In the story, men are burned at the stake and then tossed down into a deep sandy pit, left for dead but still somehow living; a dwelling place of the dead, says Kipling, "for the dead who do not die but may not live." An old Indian adage cues the text: "Alive or dead— there is no other way." In prison, in confinement, teeth falling out and health rapidly declining, Gramsci begged to differ, as apparently does Kipling, prefiguring Beckett's gloomy oeuvre by half a century. "The Strange Ride," Gramsci tells Tatiana (December 9, 1926), "immediately leaped to my mind, so much that I felt I was living it." And, again, ten days on (December 19, 1926), he repeats the message: "You must believe me when I say that my reference to Kipling's short story was not an exaggeration." (Remember, too, how Gramsci's catchphrase that "the world is great and terrible" was borrowed from the Tibetan Buddhist lama who'd starred in Kipling's *Kim*.)

Gramsci is keen to share with Delio Kipling's cheerier tales. *The Jungle Book*'s mongoose "is eaten up from nose to tail with curiosity. The motto of all the mongoose family is 'Run and find out'; and Rikki-Tikki-Tavi was a true mongoose." "I think you know the story of Kim," Gramsci writes his son (February 22, 1932); "but do you know the tales in *The Jungle Book* and especially the one about the white seal and about Rikki-Tikki-Tavi?" The latter story's climactic scene is Rikki-Tikki's showdown with the cobra Nagaina, who, along with husband Nag, had terrorized Teddy's household, the boy who'd befriended Rikki-Tikki. (Rikki-Tikki had already seen off Nag.) "Now I have Nagaina to settle with," the mongoose says, "and she will be worse than five Nags, and there's no knowing when the eggs she spoke of will hatch. Goodness!" All's well that ends well, though.

"The White Seal" features another unlikely hero from *The Jungle Book*, only his domain is the chilly high sea. The cub called Kotick grows up into a mighty white seal whose sole purpose in life is "to find a quiet island with good firm beaches for seals to live on, where men could not get at them." Other seals make fun of Kotick, with his crazy ideas of imaginary islands. Everywhere he goes, seals tell Kotick the same thing: seals had come to islands once upon a time, "but men had killed them all off." Still, one day, Kotick vows he'd lead the seal people to a quiet place. At the story's close, he roars to the seals: "I've found you the island where you'll be safe, but unless your heads are dragged off your silly necks you won't believe."

Gramsci's most famous animal story is now a children's text frequently read by teachers throughout Italy's elementary schools: *Il topo e la montagna* (*The Mouse and the Mountain*). In a letter dated June 1, 1931, Gramsci says to his wife, "I would like to tell Delio a tale from my town that seems interesting. I'll summarize it for him and Giuliano. A child is sleeping..." Gramsci begins. There's a mug of milk ready for him when he wakes up. But a mouse sneaks in and drinks the milk. In the morning, when the child opens his eyes, seeing no milk, he starts screaming. Then his mother screams.

The mouse realizes what he's done and, feeling guilty, runs to the goat to find milk. The goat will give the mouse milk if he can get grass for the goat to eat. The mouse goes into the fields looking for grass but, lacking water, the fields are all parched. The mouse goes in search of a water fountain. The fountain, however, has been ruined by war and the water is seeping out into the ground. The mouse goes to the mason, hoping he can repair the fountain, yet the mason lacks stones. The mouse goes to the mountain and then, says Gramsci, "there's a sublime dialogue between the mouse and the mountain, which has been deforested by speculators and reveals everywhere its bones stripped of earth."

Antonio Gramsci
Il topo
e la montagna

disegni di Marco Lorenzetti   Gallucci

The mouse recounts the entire story to the mountain and promises that when the child grows up, he'll replant trees on the mountain's plains. So the mountain gives the mouse stones, and the child eventually has so much milk that he can bathe in it. And when the child grows up, he does as the mouse had promised and plants trees, and everything changes: "The mountain's bones disappear under new humus, atmospheric precipitation once more becomes regular because the trees absorb the vapors and prevent torrents from devastating the plain. In short, the mouse conceives of a true and proper five-year plan. Dearest Giulia, I really want you to tell them this story and then let me know the children's impressions. I embrace you tenderly."

GRAMSCI FELT "VERY POIGNANT REGRET" ABOUT BEING AN absent father, deprived of the chance of watching his kids mature, of sharing in the development of their personalities. Perhaps he felt this regret even more than his inability to be a political man of action, something he'd strived to do, vowed since his student days in Turin. Some Gramsci scholars have pointed out this dialectic tugging away inside him, the perpetual torment between a political man and a family man, expressed in one of Gramsci's staple pieces of reading—"Canto X" of Dante's *Inferno*, the first book of *The Divine Comedy*, which Gramsci had studied off and on for more than twenty years, reading and rereading it, able to recite it from memory.

The late Frank Rosengarten, who edited and introduced Columbia University Press's wonderful two volumes of Gramsci's *Letters from Prison* (the only complete English edition), highlights Gramsci's "little discovery" with Canto X, where "two dramas" unfold: the political drama, enacted by the character Farinata, and the personal drama of Cavalcante. Gramsci wrote Tatiana on August 26, 1929: "I've made a little discovery about this canto by Dante that I believe is interesting and in part corrects Croce's thesis on *The Divine Comedy*, which is too absolute." Rosengarten says Gramsci was original and correct in his belief that everyone had overlooked the plight of Cavalcante, who, in hell, was anguished by the uncertain fate of his son, Guido.

Cavalcante's cameo plays second fiddle to the seemingly more important political tragedy of Farinata. Gramsci suggests that in Canto X Dante wasn't so much concerned with politics as with the sufferings of a heartsick father. Canto X becomes personal as well as political for Gramsci, the double commitment and tussle of a man who fought for his socialist ideals and a husband and father tormented by the forced separation from his wife and sons: "Weeping, he said to me: 'If through this blind / Prison thou goest by loftiness of genius, / Where is my son? and why is he not with thee?'" In a sense, then, we might conclude that animality speaks to both flanks of Gramsci's personality: to the libertarian thinker and to the father storyteller, protective of his offspring, displaying real gifts for narrating fables in his letters, for telling stories about animals.

That libertarian also knew another animal fable, one not yet mentioned, a strictly adult affair about *realpolitik*, about Machiavelli's Centaur—the half-human, half-animal figure with its dual powers. "You must understand," says Gramsci, quoting Machiavelli's *The Prince*, "that there are two ways of fighting: by the law and by force. The first way is natural to men, the second to beasts." Any successful movement, Gramsci believes, again following Machiavelli, must be able to assume both the nature of humans and beasts, the nature of the fox as well as that of the lion: "For while the latter cannot escape the traps laid for him, the former cannot defend himself against the wolves." The strategic ferocity of the lion and the tactical cunning of the fox, a blend of force and consent, of coercion and persuasion, exists in the struggle for a popular left hegemony.

Machiavelli, of course, says nothing about mongooses, yet for Gramsci this sort of animality meant fatherly urging, encouraging his sons to think critically while always keeping their imaginations alive, getting "eaten up from nose to tail with curiosity" like Kipling's Rikki-Tikki-Tavi, sniffing about for adventure, always being inquisitive, wanting to know why, forever "running and finding out." A little lesson in everyday life that one—not only for kids and other animals, but for grown-up humans, too.

THE GENERAL IS OUT AND ABOUT ON PATROL TODAY, ON duty again, pacing around Gramsci, doing his drills, his rounds of surveillance, ensuring that all's well. It's a lovely, bright, autumn morning, cool relief from the summer's heat. A sweet light strikes upon Gramsci's tomb, as it so often does. The General—let's relabel him "Gramsci's cat"—seems as content as ever as another cemetery day begins its quiet course. Perhaps he won't mind if I cite to him, gently under my breath, a few lines from Dante's

Canto X, as Gramsci might have liked: "Now onward goes, along
a narrow path / Between the torments and the city wall, / My
master, and I follow at his back."

I sit on Gramsci's bench and watch Gramsci's cat strut back
and forth along the narrow path, between his master and the
Aurelian city wall, and remember that the drama of Canto X actually takes place in a cemetery. "The people who are lying in these
tombs, / Might they be seen?" Suddenly, Gramsci's cat leaps
onto my lap, rubbing his head against my chest. If you sit here
long enough, calmly enough, and are respectful enough toward
Gramsci, he'll surely do the same for you. I begin to stroke him,
my hands ruffling through his thick fur. "Be pleased to stay thy
footsteps in this place," we say to each other, unspoken. I'm communing with a cat and a dead Marxist in soft Roman sunshine,
trying to keep alive our conversation, and thinking that maybe
I'm beginning to get what *animality* might really mean.

4

GOBLIN

It's easy to miss the Fondazione Gramsci, tucked away off the
street in a little building along Via Sebino, at number 43A, in
Rome's Trieste neighborhood. Its glass-door entrance lies at the
end of a discreet courtyard, modestly beyond the gaze of any
undiscerning passersby. On the afternoon of my visit—a mild,
gray, late January day—things were brightened by the warm wel-
come I received. I said I was a big Gramsci fan, had written a
few things about him, was embarked on an offbeat book about
him, about his life and thought, about him dead and alive, and I
came curious about the Fondazione's resources. I'd heard about
their extensive library, crammed with every leftist book under the
sun, in scores of languages, which I now saw filling the glassed-
in cabinets on the walls of the main *biblioteca*. I said I wanted to
tap Gramsci's digital archive as well, especially those legendary
prison notebooks, the real thing, which I knew were housed in a
special vault somewhere on the Fondazione's premises.

Those premises reminded me a lot of the long-lost Brecht
Forum in New York that I knew two decades ago—the same
low-tech shabbiness, a bit worn and grungy. The array of tatty

desktops harked back to another era, somehow bygone, pre-Apple. The Fondazione's young librarian came over to assist me, going out of her way to log me in to the system's database, telling me in perfect English that she had digitized much of the Gramsci material, all to be scrutinized without cost or subscription, with a clarity that almost lets you smudge your own fingers in Gramsci's ink. Working so intimately with Gramsci's writings must have been very exciting, I say to her. She smiled. "Yes," she said, "it was." She loves her job.

Now, we can inspect for ourselves Gramsci's meticulous note-books, his perfectly legible cursive, his precise crossings-out, done with exactitude, with a ruler, diagonal lines methodically scoring out words, sometimes whole pages; Gramsci added and eliminated text with characteristic calculation. His handwriting is so neat, so error-free, that we know it represents ideas and material already worked through, already drafted out in rough beforehand. Here we have "special," self-copyedited, clean versions of his thought, preserved for immortality.

Gramsci was finicky about the type of notebook he wanted. He wrote his sister-in-law Tatiana (February 22, 1932), "Can you send me some notebooks, but not like the ones you sent me a while ago, which are too cumbersome and too large; you should choose notebooks of a normal format like those used in school, and not too many pages, at the most forty or fifty, so that they are not inevitably transformed into increasingly jumbled miscellaneous tomes. I would like to have smaller notebooks for the purpose of collating these notes, dividing them by subject, and so once and for all putting them in order. This will help me pass the time and will be useful to me personally in achieving a certain intellectual order."

Each notebook bears on its cover the imprint "*Gius. Laterza & Figli*"—Giuseppe Laterza & Sons, a Bari-based family business, a stationer and publisher (still around to this day). Some covers are ornately designed with elaborate art deco patterning; a few have images of ancient Egypt; all have front labelling marked with Gramsci's prison number, 7047, together with a sentence he wrote indicating the subject matter inside. After Gramsci's death, Tatiana glued another marker on the upper-right-hand side, deeming each notebook either "*Completo*" or "*Incompleto*," while assigning them Roman numerals. The bulk of the note-books are roughly 6 x 8 inches in size, containing 97 leaves with twenty-one, single-spaced lines on each sheet. The parsimonious Gramsci wasted nothing, filling up both sides of the page.

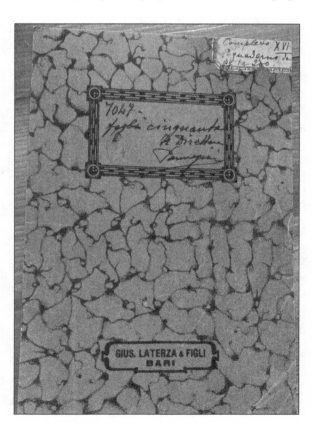

A few notebooks are larger format, 8 x 10.5 inches, and in one atypical case, *Quaderno XXXI* from 1932, he used an artist's sketchpad, 9 x 6 inches, blank-paged, with a beautiful deco *Album Disegno* frontispiece, marked "*Incompleto*" by Tatiana. Gramsci singled out here his translation of the Brothers Grimm's tale about a little goblin called "Rumpelstilzchen" (retaining its original German spelling), copying it out in neat, corrected form. Intended as a gift to his sister Teresina's children in Ghilarza, the write-up was never completed, even though Gramsci had finished the translation two years earlier, appearing in full alongside other Brothers Grimm stories in *Quaderno B* (XV).

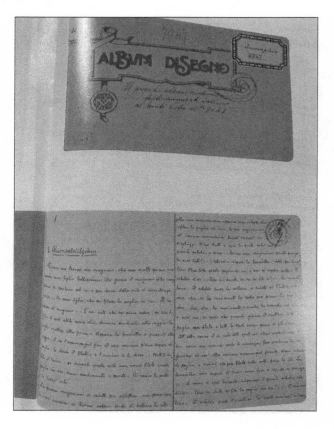

Gramsci told Teresina (January 18, 1932): "I've translated from German, as an exercise, a series of popular tales, exactly like the ones we liked so much when we were children and that actually resemble them to some extent, because their origin is the same. They're a bit old-fashioned, homespun, but modern life, with the radio, airplane, the talkies . . . has still not penetrated Ghilarza deeply enough for the taste of today's children to be very different from ours at that time. I'll make sure to copy them in a notebook and send them to you as soon as I get permission, as a contribution to the imagination of the little ones. Perhaps the person who reads them will have to add a pinch of irony and indulgence in presenting them to the listeners, as a concession to modernity."

Gramsci gives pride of place to Rumpelstiltskin, labelling the eponymous protagonist "*coboldo*" and not the "*tremotino*" used in more standard Italian translations. "*Coboldo*," from the Latin *cobalus* (meaning "rogue"), comes close to the English "kobold," from pagan mythology, a hobgoblin who haunts households and plays mischievous tricks, especially if it feels neglected or offended; Gramsci says the tale reminded him of the Sardinian folkloric legends that had kindled his own homespun island imagination. If anything, Gramsci physically resembled the deformed goblin—tiny, less than five feet tall, and hunch-backed; both, too, were outsiders and pariahs with mischievous, stubborn streaks. Remember that the dwarfed Gramsci was bullied terribly at school and remember that in prison he refused to plead for clemency, seeing it as a capitulation to fascism, a kind of moral suicide, an implicit admission that he'd recanted his Marxist views. In this sense, the frank, if austere, goblin way spoke personally to the sly and stoic Gramsci, appealed to him as a state of being in the capitalist world.

Rumpelstiltskin said his name was unusual and Gramsci sometimes said his own name was unusual, too. Is your name "Gasparo, Mechiore, Baldassare?" the queen asked the goblin in Gramsci's translation. "Is it Gatarino, Saltamontore, Tombatore? Giovanni or Giuseppe?" In "my journey through this 'great and terrible world,'" Gramsci tells Tatania (February 19, 1927), "I'm not known outside a rather restricted circle; therefore my name is mangled in the most unlikely ways: Gramasci, Granusci, Gramisci, even Garamascon, with all the most bizarre in-betweens."

The goblin, like Gramsci, is portrayed as the villain, when the real villains—the miller, his daughter, the king—are presented as good and upright; it's they who live happily ever after. And yet, Rumpelstiltskin is the only honest soul among them, the only character true to his word. The miller is a liar who gives his daughter away to the king. The miller says she can spin straw into gold, which she can't. The king, who's nasty and greedy, is impressed. He carts her off and locks her up in a dungeon with a spinning wheel. If she can turn the piles of straw into gold then he'll marry her; if not, it's off with her head. The king is excited at the prospect of so much wealth and will stop at nothing to get it. "I'll be back in the morning for the gold," he says. As night falls, the girl is at a loss living up to her father's conceited promise. She starts to cry.

Suddenly, a funny little goblin appears, asking the reason for her tears. He listens with a sympathetic ear. After she explains, he laughs. "Is that all? Why, I can do that in a twinkle," he says nonchalantly. For him, you don't have to be very clever to spin lots of gold (they do it all the time on the stock market, spinning yarn and yarns all the way to the bank); nor do you have to work particularly hard. Rumpelstiltskin knows that making lots of money is no big deal, that there are other paradigms to life, other less venal and more magical ways to find fulfillment. He spins the gold in return for the girl's pretty necklace.

Next morning, the king is delighted. That evening, Rumpelstiltskin returns and spins more gold, this time in exchange for the girl's ring. The king, again, is thrilled. On the third evening, the miller's daughter has nothing more to give the goblin, so she promises him her firstborn child. This time, he fills the whole room with gold, and the king goes wild with excitement and marries the girl that very same day. The kingdom rejoices at the marriage and later at the birth of the queen's beautiful daughter.

When the goblin hears the news, he comes back for the baby. "Remember," he says, "there was an agreement, and you're bound by that." The queen weeps, gets down on her knees, begs him not to take her baby away. Again, the goblin sympathizes, and says, "All right, my name is unusual, if you can guess it, you're released from the promise." He'll be back tomorrow, he says. But the queen plays crooked and sends a servant to snoop and find out his name. A while later, the servant returns, grinning all over. "I followed him to a little shack, deep in the forest, and there I heard him singing his song, and he bawled out his name." Next morning, the goblin reappears before the queen. She utters his name and, "spitting and squealing, he vanished out of the window like a balloon when you take your fingers off the nozzle." Nothing is ever heard of him again. Meanwhile, the king, the queen, and the young princess live happily . . . blah, blah, blah.

This warped and shallow value system is inculcated in us early. If you follow its rules, you get rewarded accordingly. You'll live happily ever after, not rot in jail. But the reality of the tale is that its winners do everything we know a ruling class does: it lies and cheats, boasts and breaks deals, spies on you if need be, and always sends others to do its dirty work. Moreover, it rarely keeps its word. The queen breaks her compact. The king has no other interest than accumulating wealth; he doesn't even love the woman he married. Everybody is duplicitous and conniving. They're all phony schemers, out to extract something from somebody else—all except the ugly goblin Rumpelstiltskin.

In all, Gramsci translated twenty-four Brothers Grimm tales (actually twenty-three, with one unfinished piece). They've since been collected together under the rubric *Favole di libertà: La fiabe dei Fratelli Grimm tradotte in carcere*, implying that if your body is incarcerated, then there are other possibilities to reimagine a liberty of the mind, a liberty of the imagination; and Gramsci seems drawn to fairy tales for these motives. He knew the Brothers Grimm's work was firmly rooted in German folklore, just as his own Marxism was rooted in Italian folklore, in its culture and regionalism, in its "non-official" *subaltern* tradition.

Some of Gramsci's translations are done for personal amusement; others as offerings to nephews and nieces who never knew Uncle Antonio. Despite the simplicity and naivety of the tales, Gramsci thought there was something here for adults, too, something *political* about folkloric tales, about their function within a particular oppressed stratum of society; an *educative* element, which is why, in *Quaderno 27* (XI), he devotes singular attention to "observations on folklore" (*Osservazioni sul folclore*). Gramsci suggests folklore should be studied as "a conception of the world and life implicit to a large strata of society, in opposition to 'official' conceptions of the world." It has, he says, "sturdy historical roots" and "is tenaciously entwined in the psychology of specific popular strata."

Gramsci, as ever, is dialectical, conceiving folklore critically and inquisitively, not narrow-mindedly. "Folklore mustn't be considered an eccentricity," he insists, "as an oddity or a picturesque element, but as something which is very serious and is to be taken seriously." And he takes it seriously, even while he sometimes laughs out loud. He acknowledges its ties with religion and superstition, to "crude and mutilated thought." Nonetheless, with folklore, "one must distinguish various strata," Gramsci says, "the fossilized ones which reflect conditions of past life and are therefore conservative and reactionary, and those which consist of a series of innovations, often creative and progressive, determined spontaneously by forms of life which are in the process of developing, in contradiction to the morality of the governing strata." "Only in this way," he says, "will the teaching of folklore be more efficient and really bring about the birth of a new culture among the broad popular masses."

AS I WAS LEAVING THE FONDAZIONE GRAMSCI, THE YOUNG librarian urged me to help myself to Gramsci paraphernalia on a bookshelf near the door, to books and pamphlets, as well as to wonderful Fondazione-produced postcards of the covers of *Quaderni del carcere*, in gleaming color. It was a treasure trove of Gramscian regalia. I wasted no time packing my shoulder bag with a big-formatted Fondazione publication called *Antonio Gramsci e la grande Guerra*, lavishly illustrated with fascinating reproductions of pre-prison Gramsci letters (from 1915 to 1916), on *Avanti! (Edizione Torinese)*-headed notepaper. I also bagged an interesting French booklet titled *Les cahiers de prison et la France*, together with a text, *Gramsci in Gran Bretagna*, discussing the reception of Gramsci in the UK, notably the brilliant reinterpretations of Eric Hobsbawm, Perry Anderson, and Stuart Hall. And, needless to say, I grabbed a stash of those glossy postcards.

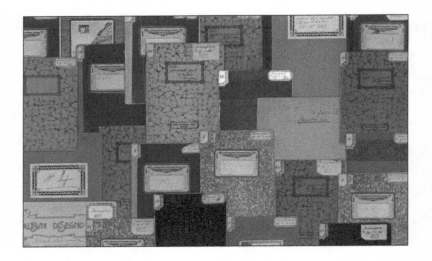

Exiting, and reflecting upon what I'd just seen in the archive, I realized how much of what Gramsci wrote was really about self-expression, about collecting and collating his own thoughts, putting them in intellectual order, clarifying his own position, often vis-à-vis an antagonist. Before his arrest, Gramsci saw himself as a journalist-activist. He never wrote elaborate tomes, extended monographs, never had any inclination to do so. His writings were short, pithy, quickly drafted political interventions, polemical engagements with the urgency of the moment.

"In ten years of journalism," he told Tatiana (September 7, 1931), "I wrote enough lines to fill fifteen or twenty volumes of 400 pages each, but they were written for the day and, in my opinion, were supposed to die with the day. I have always refused to permit publication of a collection of them, even a limited one." In 1918, an Italian publisher wanted to publish his *Avanti!* articles, with "a friendly and laudatory preface . . . but I refused to allow it," Gramsci says. A couple of years on, he apparently had a change of heart, letting Giuseppe Prezzolini's publishing house convince him to issue a collection of newspaper pieces. But then suddenly got cold feet and told Tatiana, "I chose to pay the cost of the part of the type already set and withdrew the manuscript."

All the same, a major component of those writings, both inside and outside prison, had an explicit pedagogical intent: that of popularizing Marxism, of trying to communicate socialist ideas with an immediacy that resonated with a wider, lay public, sometimes with an immediacy that resonated with Gramsci himself. Large tracks of the prison notebooks were really thoughts toward Gramsci's own version of a "Popular Manual of Marxism," doubtless in mind when musing on folklore and common sense, and certainly in mind when launching his "critical notes" against Bukharin's "Popular Manual." The "Popular Manual" was Gramsci's shorthand for Nikolai Bukharin's *Theory of Historical Materialism: A Popular Manual of Marxist Sociology*, published in Moscow in 1921. What disappointed Gramsci most of all here was its missed opportunity: the book's promising subtitle bore scant resemblance to its contents.

Bukharin's position expressed the vulgar materialism of the era, Gramsci says, reducing Marxism to a positivist (and positive) science. (In the 1930s, Bukharin himself became a skeptic of Stalin's regime, opposed the first Five-Year Plan and the collectivization of agriculture. Accused of conspiracy, a show trial found him guilty. He was executed in 1938.) Bukharin, says Gramsci, began all wrongly, and "should have taken as his starting point a critical analysis of the philosophy of common sense." Common sense, says Gramsci, "is the folklore of philosophy, and, like folklore, takes countless different forms." Common sense needs transcending, not wholesale rejection. It's the breeding ground of good sense, of a materialism much more realistic and a lot richer than Bukharin's, something both critical and curious, open and ironic, maybe even folkloric—a mischievous "goblin" sort of

Marxism that speaks the twisted language of ordinary people, for better or for worse.

One thing surely not lost on Gramsci when translating the Brothers Grimm is how god-awful their characters are, how scheming and duplicitous, how untruthful and dishonest. Some Grimm tales are just that: *grim*, darn-right nasty, and their moral message is hard to grasp—if, indeed, there is any moral message to grasp. It's like reading the daily news. You know, "Once upon a time there was a nasty ex-President who wanted to seize power again..." Maybe that's Gramsci's point? That life actually is "great and terrible," and only by confronting its pitfalls and perils, its terrors and turmoil head on, never capitulating before its nastiness, can we hope to maximize a great that's increasingly hard to see. And sometimes you need to laugh at it.

Pessimism or optimism? Gramsci probably wouldn't have framed it as such, never would have conceived our world nowadays so dualistically, so either/or. This is him talking in 1929, powerfully articulating his position to younger brother Carlo: "Humans bear within themselves the source of their own moral strength, that everything depends on us, on our energy, on our will, on the iron coherence of the aims that we set ourselves and the means we adopt to realize them, that we will never again despair and lapse into those vulgar, banal states of mind that are pessimism and optimism. My state of mind synthesizes these two emotions and overcomes them." Gramsci's fairy tales, we might say, spin yarns about the realm of Marxist necessity.

5

SUBALTERN

Gramsci saw the whole of the Italian "South" as a kind of goblin, as a character who, like Rumpelstiltskin, got and kept getting a bad rap. In late 1926, a month or so prior to his arrest, he was at work on a long essay about the Italian South, *Alcuni temi della questione Meridionale—Some Aspects on the Southern Question.* The piece was never completed; it was rudely interrupted; and while there's a lot left dangling, there's plenty for us still to glean. Gramsci was addressing his Marxist comrades, notably comrades from the north, in a tone that's critical, inquiring, taking to task all camps, typically trying to get at the truth—warts and all. Gramsci chastised a right northern bourgeoisie as well as a left industrial proletariat, northern Marxists as well as southern liberals, workers from the north as well as gentry from the south.

Point is that all of this is voiced by a lad from the south. Gramsci's political awakening occurred in the north, yet his cultural allegiances always rested with the south. He grew up in peasant society, spoke local Ghilarza dialect, and probably didn't hear formal Italian until he reached grammar school, and then, in Turin, through his college professors. As a poor, set-apart kid, encountering official Italian was likely both a source of liberation and a lesson in officialdom, the tenor of a ruling-class authority he was out to smash.

So part of Gramsci's struggle was to invent not only a different kind of Marxism but also a different kind of language, a different political register that spoke neither raw dialect nor elitist Italian. In a sense, amalgamating the two interested the linguist in him, mixing the language of the countryside with that of the city, reconciling the expressive powers of vernacular with the sobriety of reason, converting a common sense into good sense; a Marxism neither flaky idealism nor iron-law materialism yet something else again—a concrete, authentic, philosophy of praxis sensitive to place, culture, and tradition. There's a lot more *there* there in Gramsci's Marxism.

We can witness this flowing through "Some Aspects on the Southern Question." He's especially skeptical of how his factory council comrades want to resolve southern "backwardness." By smashing the capitalist factory autocracy, they say, smashing an oppressive state apparatus, a workers' state would then smash the chains that bind peasants to the land. Taking over industry and the banks would swing the enormous weight of the state bureaucracy behind the peasants, helping them vanquish in their struggle against southern landowners.

Gramsci doesn't buy into this northern patronage, into the communist "magical formula" (as he labels it). He doesn't believe the solution to the "Southern Question" lies in the hands of a northern workers' vanguard. Northern communists, he says, have more in common with their bourgeois antagonists, much more than they consciously appreciate. They've been "unconsciously subjected to the influence of bourgeois education, to bourgeois press, to bourgeois traditions."

"It's well known," Gramsci says, "what kind of ideology has been disseminated in myriad ways among the masses in the north, by propagandists of the bourgeoisie: the south is the ball and chain which prevents the social development of Italy from progressing more rapidly; southerners are biologically inferior beings, semi-barbarians or total barbarians, by natural destiny; if the South is backward, the fault doesn't lie with the capitalist system, but with nature, which has made southerners lazy, incapable, criminal and barbaric."

Left-wing positivism has often reinforced southern inferiority: "Science was used to crush the wretched and exploited, but this time it was dressed in socialist colors and claimed to be the science of the proletariat." Factory workers and Marxist intellectuals, Gramsci says, have to rethink this approach so that the left can become politically effective throughout all Italy. Proletarians and their leaders "must strip themselves of every residue of corporatism, every syndicalist prejudice and incrustation," he says. They need to overcome distinctions between one trade and another, between factory workers and artisans, industrial laborers and toilers on the land, between the city and the countryside—between a north and south embedded in people's heads.

Spatial antagonisms—urban versus rural, north versus south, etc.—tend to occlude basic class questions, says Gramsci, and one of the biggest problems here is *organizing*. In the south, urban forces are subordinate to rural forces, the city kowtows to the countryside. In the Mezzogiorno, the countryside is less progressive than the city; but southern urbanism, unlike its northern counterpart, isn't industrial, and can't be organized in the same fashion as a giant car plant; the culture and history of Naples is different from Turin and Milan. And yet, given the dominance of the industrial north, and the greater leverage of its factory workers and unions, the latter has to convince southern rural and urban working classes that they're all brothers and sisters in the same struggle.

The schism between city and countryside, in other words, is much more nuanced than crudely meets the eye. Indeed, Gramsci warns about the ideology of appearances. "The relations between urban population and rural population," he says, "aren't a single, schematic type." Figuring out their dialectical specifics, as well as fulfilling an educative and directive role, is the task Gramsci ascribes to "organic intellectuals," a species of thinker and activist different from "traditional" intellectuals: the latter, he says, are more conciliatory—lawyers, doctors, notaries, teachers, priests, bureaucrats, and technocrats—professionals who, wittingly or unwittingly, prop up the status quo rather than tear it down. Left organic intellectuals, on the other hand, feel the elemental passions of "the people" and become "permanent persuaders." They critically explain the movement of history, as well as the working class's interests in that movement. In Italy, as elsewhere, organic intellectuals help forge a "national-popular collective will."

GRAMSCI'S HEALTH WORSENED TOWARD THE END OF 1933. Sister-in-law Tatiana and longtime Gramsci friend Piero Sraffa, a renowned economist at the University of Cambridge, made frequent appeals about getting him moved and better cared for. After Turi's prison doctor also recommended a transfer, the fascist government eventually authorized Gramsci's shift to Professor Giuseppe Cusumano's health clinic in Formia, a coastal town 100 miles south of Rome. Although still under police surveillance, Gramsci could go out for occasional short walks, accompanied by an approved individual. Every Sunday, Tatiana journeyed down by train from Rome, and together they'd walk along the beachfront; sometimes brother Carlo came, and a few times Sraffa himself, from the UK.

Gramsci's poor health, though, meant he couldn't fully

benefit from his newfound conditional liberty. A cleaner at the Cusumano clinic recalled her initial glimpse of the new patient: "Small, hunchbacked, wrapped in a black Sardinian shepherd's cloak, between two policemen." "I was disappointed," she said. "They told me Gramsci was the leader of the communists, a revolutionary, and I'd imagined him tall, imposing, not so small, minute, tired; but his eyes were clear, alive, penetrating, they dug into you. It was clear he was an extraordinary man."

Significantly, Gramsci was now allowed access to *all* his notebooks at the same time—at Turi, he was only able to see five in one go. Thus he began recopying old raw notes, modifying them, expanding them here, deleting them there, collating, grouping them together into "special" single-topic themes. In July 1934, Gramsci started to assemble Notebook 25, *Ai margini della storia (storia dei gruppi sociali subalterni)—On the Margins of History (The History of Subaltern Social Groups)*—bringing his scattered writings from Turi together into a 160-page composition notebook, larger-sized than he typically used before, and a different brand—"Ditta CUGINI ROSSI ROMA."

Evidently, he'd anticipated a bigger project—on slaves and plebians from Ancient Roman and medieval Italy, on peasants and proletarians, on subaltern social groups' connection to history and economics, to common sense and folklore, to spontaneity and intellectuals—on the potential for them acquiring hegemony; developing their own autonomous political consciousness; revolting against the bourgeoisie; taking their subordination out of the realm of civil society and politicking around the state, maybe one day becoming a state themselves. There was enough material here, Gramsci felt, to constitute an extended monograph, kickstarted with that essay on the southern question almost a decade earlier. He'd left the first ten pages of Notebook 25 blank, readied for an introductory text and a summary index that, with ever-

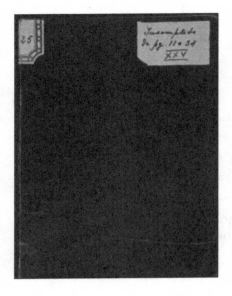

failing health, he never managed to create. Hence Tatiana marked *Quaderno 25* (XXV) *"Incompleto."*

Gramsci was an original, a chip off the old block, the first Marxist ever to mobilize the term "subaltern." He never knew it, of course, but he single-handedly invented a whole new discipline: "Subaltern Studies," with its emphasis on the ignored and neglected in Western history, as if it were the only history. Now, Gramsci's southern question has enlarged to embrace the *Global South*, a southern global imagination, those excluded "from historiography of the dominant classes, although protagonists of real history."

In 2021, Columbia University Press thought Gramsci's treatment of subaltern social groups sufficiently important to warrant English translation (by Joseph Buttigieg and Marcus Green), and a "critical edition" of Notebook 25, combining allusions to subalternity from other Gramsci notebooks. The project would compensate for the short shrift *Selections from Prison Notebooks* initially afforded the topic—with no index entry for a thematic so personally and politically vital to Gramsci, the dark-skinned, hunchbacked goblin, a pariah from a culture different than the dominant. He empathized with subalterns, knew them, recognized them, because he came from them, recognized himself in them.

"Often," Gramsci says, "subaltern groups are originally of

a different race (different religion and different culture) than dominant groups, and they're often a mixture of races…. The question of the importance of women is similar to the question of subaltern groups … 'masculinism' can be compared to class domination." Subaltern classes, he says, are portrayed "as having no history, people whose history leaves no traces in the historical documents of the past."

Subalterns have to prise themselves free from the subjection dominant forces have imposed upon them. They also have to prise themselves free from their own passivity. This is hard, Gramsci admits, because "we're all conformists of some conformism of another, always man-in-the-mass or collective man"; we all belong to a particular social grouping that transmits, for better or for worse, its own uniform mode of thinking and acting. To that degree, one needs to be hard on oneself as well as on one's antagonists; one needs to struggle against the world while struggling against oneself, internalizing at the same time as externalizing rebellion.

"When one's conception of the world isn't critical and coherent," Gramsci says, "but disjointed and episodic, one belongs to a multiplicity of mass human groups." The trick "is to criticize one's own conception of the world," to make "a coherent unity and to raise it to the level reached by the most advanced thought in the world." "The starting point of critical elaboration," he says, "is the consciousness

of what one really is, and 'knowing thyself' as a product of the historical process to date which has deposited in you an infinity of traces without leaving an inventory."

The subaltern, more than anybody else, needs to know themselves connected to the historical process, know themselves as being on the receiving end of this process, know how they've been undermined by that process, and sometimes how they've undermined themselves in that process. One problem is that even when subalterns rebel, "they're in a state of anxious defense." "Every trace of autonomous initiative, therefore, is of inestimable value." Gramsci captures here the perennial condition of the modern left: *in a state of anxious defense.*

The other problem is that when subaltern groups aren't looked down upon, scorned and abused, they're patronized, treated as "humble." It's a characteristic attitude, Gramsci says, of a lot of intellectuals, even well-meaning ones. For the Italian intellectual, "Humble indicates a relationship of paternal protection, the 'self-sufficient' feeling of one's own undisputed superiority; like the relationship between two races, one superior, the other inferior; like the relationship between adult and child in old schooling; or, worse still, like the relationship of a 'society for the protection of animals' or like that of the Anglo-Saxon Salvation Army toward the cannibals of Papua."

It's a sensibility in stark contrast to Dostoevsky's, Gramsci says, as depicted in, for instance, *The Insulted and Injured* (1861), a novel never terribly well favored by Dostoevsky aficionados, his first after Siberian exile. But Gramsci had spotted something in it that struck a suggestive political chord. "In Dostoevsky," he says, "there's a strong national-popular feeling, namely, an awareness of a mission of the intellectual toward the people, who may be 'objectively' composed of the 'humble' but must be freed from this 'humility,' transformed and regenerated."

Gramsci doesn't mention it by name, but this idea of "a mission of the intellectual toward the people" emerged in Russia during the early 1860s, expressed most fervently in the Narodnik movement. Young progressive urban intellectuals, dressed in simple peasant garb, fled cities and went "to the people," canvassing across the countryside, inciting revolt against tsarist rule. They lived among the people, merged with the people, taught them, learned from them, and tried to fight for their collective interests. Gramsci saw in the Narodniks a model for catalyzing revolt, a prototypical representation of the organic intellectual, somebody who could help the subaltern speak without ever putting words in their mouths.

THE CUSUMANO CLINIC WAS A DREADFUL PLACE FOR Gramsci. His letters indicate shoddy treatment. Tatiana claimed her brother-in-law's health went further downhill. He had to endure incompetent medical care, she said, inedible food, and no hot water for bathing. He suffered the "neglect, indifference, indolence" of the clinic's staff. Tatiana was damning. Adding to existing health woes, Gramsci developed a hernia, requiring the surgery he never got. His nervous and digestive systems were kaput. He was feverish, seized by tremors. Even holding a pen was a chore. Urinal infections meant frequently pissing blood.

And he couldn't sleep: "The Cusumano family has arrived," he told Tatiana (July 22, 1935). "Over my head there's a continuous to and fro from five in the morning until midnight. . . . I'm a sick person and every slightest rustle agitates me enormously. I will recover from many ailments and precisely from those which at the moment are the most tormenting." "I am absolutely determined," he added, "to leave the Cusumano clinic and as soon as possible."

I was intrigued about this clinic in Formia, long since shut down. I understood that the building still stood, overlooking the

beach, and so, one Sunday morning in early March, on an unsea-
sonably blustery, rainy day, I got into my car and made the two-
hour drive down from Rome. Waves crashed into Formia's water-
front wall; walking the half a mile or so from the center of town,
along Via Appia Lato Napoli, toward number 30, necessitated
a salty sea-spray drenching. Then the former clinic appeared, a
standalone five-story cream structure, a lot smaller than I'd imagined, with decorative pink cornices, green shutters, and small
balconies. Once it would have had a certain grandeur, an archi-
tecture suggesting 1920s construction. In Gramsci's day, it would
have felt almost new. In our day, it's a condo apartment complex,
opposite a gas station. Although occupied, most of the windows
are shuttered, maybe for the season, and overall the place strikes
one as in need of a little care and attention, a rehab and refresh.

I peered through a glass main doorway, into a tired-looking
entrance foyer, with plant pots and ornately patterned brown
tiling. Doubtless the exact same flooring once walked upon by
Gramsci, wrapped in his Sardinian shepherd's shawl. A large
arched window at the far end, with traces of its former splendor,
opens onto the sea, offering an impressive view; yet, again, today,

everything seems worn and musty, its better days behind. At the upper right of the entrance doorway, on the outside wall, a faded marble plaque, inaugurated on April 27, 1945, the eighth anniversary of Gramsci's death, commemorates his miserable Formia sojourn.

The surrounding grounds, a parkland full of abandoned olive trees, has fallen into rack and ruin, with overgrown grass and weeds, rotting, up-ended paddle boats, and rusty marine equipment. It's inexplicable how run down everything is. In other circumstances, it might have been a mini paradise by the sea. Gramsci and Tatiana would have strolled around this patch sometimes. "I've seen some little boys catching fish in the sea," Gramsci said, in an undated letter to Guilia, one of only a handful written from Formia.

The letter is quoted on another plaque commemorating Gramsci, at a park along Via Giuseppe Verdi—*Parco di Gramsci*— a few minutes on foot from the old clinic. The greenspace's centerpiece is a large marble bust of the man himself, in his younger days, without glasses, looking like a Greek god, dating from April 27, 2000, the sixty-third anniversary of Gramsci's passing. There are two granite writing tablets below, again Greek-style. One says

Gramsci was "locked up by the fascist regime, gravely ill, at the Cusumano clinic in Formia, from December 7, 1933 to August 24, 1935," concluding with the infamous words of the public prosecutor at Gramsci's mock trial: "For twenty years we must prevent this brain from functioning."

The adjacent tablet cites his letter about the kids fishing on Formia's beach, accompanied with words to son Delio, from a 1936 letter: "I think you like history just as I did when I was your age, because it deals with human beings. And everything that deals with people, as many people as possible, all the people in the world as they join together in society and work and struggle and better themselves should please you more than anything else . . . I embrace you, Papa."

Gramsci's Park, alas, resembles Gramsci's former clinic: jaded and shoddy, falling apart. Maybe it's just the inclement

weather, but everywhere around here seems desolate, uncared for, graffiti-splattered. The park's furniture and kids' playground need an overhaul. By all accounts, the site was in an even worse state of disrepair a decade ago. For a while back then it was closed for renewal. But the refurbishment hasn't worn well, and today the park looks a lot like it did in those former days. One image, published in the local newspaper *Latina24*, from 2014, shows Gramsci's bust scarily daubed with a swastika, and it reminded me of the desecration of Marx's Highgate grave in 2019.

It's hard to know what's being remonstrated here. Is it that local Nazis didn't like Gramsci? Or is it that the perpetrators thought Gramsci was a Nazi? Both are hard to square. Both disturb with their wanton ignorance—though, of course, Nazis aren't usually known for their smarts. The other thing that disturbs is that the culprits probably hailed from the subaltern classes that Gramsci singles out; someone excluded, unemployed, alienated, having

little going on in their lives, with dismal future prospects, and a present full of discontentment. Their resentment prefers lashing out rightward. You'd have thought we'd learned our lesson from the past.

Walking back into town, dampened by the weather and by what I'd seen, feeling a bit dismal myself, I began musing on Gramsci's subaltern social groups, on what it might mean nowadays. A week or so prior to my visiting Formia, I'd read a piece in the *New York Times* (February 26, 2024), "The Mystery of White Rural Rage," by Paul Krugman, about rural America, about the baffling political backlash of rural populations. Agricultural employment has declined, and small-town manufacturing has all but collapsed. American farms produce five times more than they did seventy-five years ago with two-thirds less employment. The United States has become richer from agriculture, yet rural areas have become a lot poorer. Employment opportunities have dwindled and a loss of dignity around work sets the tone for many rural dwellers, the majority of whom are white.

Anger is voiced against the federal government and urban America. Poor city minorities and immigrants have been favored over hardworking white Americans, they say, even though federal programs helping poor rural areas—Social Security, Medicare, and Medicaid—are disproportionately financed by urban areas. Hence there's actually a de facto net transfer from urban to rural areas. Paul Krugman wonders why, instead of supporting Joe Biden, who has generally been favorable to rural America, bilious rage gives the thumbs up to Donald Trump—"a huckster from Queens, who," says Krugman, "offers little other than validation of their resentment."

It's a curious reinvention of Gramsci's "southern question." Only now the southerners in question are those not only geographically southern, but culturally southern, too, people from the periphery who feel that periphery inside them, their own peripheralization from the core, from the north, from urban areas, as if their history is getting overlooked. Occluded in the process are, as Gramsci had it, basic questions of class, of why poor "southerners" don't identify with poor "northern" folk, yet instead endorse a rich northern real estate fraudster. It's beguiling. The other point is how subalternity takes on different skin hues—populations that, to greater or lesser degrees, are now marked by outsiderness, by exclusion and neglect, a feeling that their history and culture isn't acknowledged by the perceived powers that be.

Gramsci's southern question essay hoped for a left turn in southern sensibility. Yet current climes suggest otherwise, that certain subalterns value more the visceral bleat of the right. Krugman reckons white rural rage "is arguably the single greatest threat facing American democracy," and laments, "I've no good ideas about how to fight it." Meantime, white rural working classes give gung-ho support to politicians who tell them the lies they seemingly want to hear—to those who're the real threat facing American democracy. Gramsci knew about baffling reactionary politics, about how, sometimes, many subalterns end up voting for politicians and programs that go against their better interests. He tried to tell people the truth and got locked up for it.

Marxists once used to talk about "false consciousness," the obverse of "knowing thyself." For decades, false consciousness went out of fashion, yet lately it's well and truly back in vogue, assuming an almost objective status, blurring reality and make-believe, so entrenched has it become in our society, so ubiquitous in our mass and social media, so commonplace in the misinformation sprouted by our politicians. All of it conspires to convey an implicitly distorted sense of reality, handy for vested political and economic interests—like it always did. A form of widespread brainwashing, where it's easier to be believed for peddling lies than for telling the honest truth.

Gramsci emphasized the need for intellectuals to correct misconception, to persist in telling the truth, to go and voice it to the people. But maybe intellectuals have turned away from the people, just as the people have turned away from intellectuals. Maybe we've let the people down, retreated to our college campuses, given ourselves over to management committees and research assessments. We've been busier raising money rather than raising a ruckus. We've been bought off by the good life or else gotten complacent.

Or maybe a lot of us have simply gotten depressed about a left always being in "a state of anxious defense," forever on the back-foot, or more often entirely lame, and we're happier sitting behind our desks writing stuff like this. Organic intellectuals have gone elsewhere for nourishment, turned traditional. Or perhaps the most effective "permanent persuaders" have been those on the right flank, relentlessly inveigling people that lying is the winning ticket, that crank demagogues will really make things great again.

And yet, and yet, Gramsci continues to inspire, come what may. At least he inspires me, and the countless people of all nationalities I've seen coming to the cemetery to pay their respects. He especially inspires in these dire circumstances because he was a Marxist who'd made dire circumstances something of a specialty. The idea that things might get better, that people matter, that not everybody is innately bad or a fool, that the truth will prevail in the end, is what he never ceased to endorse. It's a belief system that comes without guarantees, and often Gramsci made statements that were positive but then tinged them with doubts and caveats, with criticisms of criticisms. "Everything that deals with people," we can remember him telling his son, "as many people as possible, all the people in the world as they join together in society and work and struggle and better themselves should please you more than anything else. But is it like that?"

I really hope it is.

6

A FRIEND

I was in New York recently, where I once lived some twenty years back, there to visit my old friend and mentor, my old university teacher—and now he *is* old—an eighty-nine-year-old David Harvey, the world-renowned Marx scholar. I hadn't seen him for a while and was keen to catch up, to hear his news and tell him some of my own, about my life in Rome, about my work on Gramsci. Ever so brilliant, it's good to get some tips from David, some inspiration, a little encouragement, as well as a bit of critical feedback. As usual, too, in his company, we did a lot of talking and eating, some drinking, and together we rode the East River ferry over to Brooklyn and back, just for the fun of it, on a bitterly cold afternoon. It's one of David's favorite Big Apple pastimes; he does it alone most days; during Covid lockdowns, he said, it was an al fresco lifeline.

David is always working on some book or another and his latest is *The Story of Capital*, another iteration bringing Marx alive, of showing how the great bearded prophet can still help us understand our very troubled world. "The duty of the author," says David in the book's "mission" statement, "is to create an audience rather than to satisfy one. When Marx wrote most workers were illiterate. The audience he sought to shape was comprised largely of self-educated artisans in the throes of transformation into industrial labor. Marx sought to teach them that another world of laboring and living might be possible…. In this book," David says, "the perspective of the emancipated worker will be our helpmate and guide."

During our conversations, we got into the subject of Gramsci and his friend Piero Sraffa, whom David remembers from his undergraduate days in the mid-1950s at St. John's College, Cambridge, whose grounds were next to Trinity's, where Sraffa had a research fellowship. These days, David forgets plenty of things he did last week, but he vividly remembers seeing Sraffa well over half a century ago. He still holds the image of a middle-aged man standing, hands behind his back, staring at a twentysomething David and his pals playing tennis. Sraffa bizarrely held his gaze, appeared rather odd, like another eccentric Cambridge type. Afterward, wondering just who was this strange character staring at them, he was informed it was none other than Piero Sraffa, the famous Italian economist, friend of an even more famous economist, John Maynard Keynes, and of an equally eccentric (and famous) philosopher called Ludwig Wittgenstein—and, of course, Sraffa was Antonio Gramsci's final friend, an ever loyal friend, the only friend Gramsci had at the end of his life, one of the last people to see Gramsci alive. There he stood standing, looking at a young English Geography undergraduate who, decades later, living in New York, was destined to become a famous interpreter of Karl Marx.

David spoke about Sraffa's economics, about his stellar reputation, about him never publishing much, about his magnum opus, *The Production of Commodities by Means of Commodities*, from 1960, a rather slim deal, barely reaching a hundred pages, filled with as many simultaneous equations as actual written text.

Sraffa was, by all accounts, a brilliant mathematician and logician, with a razor-sharp mind. Wittgenstein, no slouch at the intelligence stakes himself, said that after talking with Sraffa he felt like a tree that had just had its branches hacked off, pruned for its own good.

Yet, as a writer, Sraffa seemed forever blocked, finding it difficult to lay words down on the page, no matter what the language, whether in native Italian or adopted English. (He's reputed to have begun *The Production of Commodities* in 1926!) He knew this, too, was painfully aware of it, confessing to Gramsci's sister-in-law Tatiana (August 23, 1931) that "in the past Nino [Gramsci] always chided me for having too many scientific scruples, saying that this stopped me from writing anything: I have never been cured of that illness." Ironically, Sraffa sometimes threw this judgment back in Nino's face, criticizing his work on the history of Italian intellectuals, joking that his friend was likewise crippled with those same "scruples," wanting to read everything before he could say anything.

And Gramsci admitted as much to Tatiana (August 3, 1931), in a tone not unreminiscent of Piero's: "You must remember that the habit of rigorous philological discipline acquired during my years at the university imbued me, perhaps excessively, with methodological scruples." Tatiana didn't contradict her brother-in-law: "You used to rebuke Piero constantly for his excessive scientific scruples that prevented him from writing anything; it seems that he has never cured himself of this illness, but is it possible that ten years of journalism have not cured you?"

With Tatiana, Sraffa was the gossamer thread that connected Gramsci to the outside world. Sraffa co-managed Gramsci's bureaucratic and administrative affairs; regularly visited his friend in confinement; picked up the tab for his friend's medical bills (like the costs of Formia and Quisisana clinics); brought the criminality of Gramsci's brush with fascism to international attention. Sraffa was instrumental in getting a letter, "The Methods of Fascism: The Case of Antonio Gramsci," published in the *Manchester Guardian* (October 24, 1927), penned by "an Italian in England."

Piero and Nino exchanged ideas, criticized one another, encouraged each other; Nino often used Piero, seven years his junior, as an intellectual sounding board, as a trusted interlocutor, asking for advice, for suggestions, whether his friend could chase down a source, a book or journal, a magazine or newspaper article, could he confirm this or that fact, find out some precise detail about Croce's historical studies, if Machiavelli ever wrote anything about economics, or David Ricardo about philosophy. Sraffa opened an account at a Milan bookstore, Sterling & Kupfer, from which Gramsci obtained unlimited numbers of books, as many as he was allowed on the inside.

Sraffa secured Gramsci a subscription to the *Manchester Guardian*, which Gramsci read with intent, practicing his English, preferring the northern broadsheet to the London *Times*: "London stands to Rome as Manchester to Milan," he told Tatiana (January 26, 1931), "and the difference appears also in the weekly publications. Those of London are too full of weddings and births of lords and ladies and by comparison I still prefer pages about the cultivation of cotton in northern Egypt." Gramsci asked Tatiana to write Sraffa, telling him: "I am making rapid progress in reading English; it is much easier for me than German. I read fairly rapidly."

Sraffa, meantime, became an intermediary between Gramsci and the exiled PCI leadership, bivouacking in Paris; and he made trips to Moscow to see Gramsci's wife and sons, relaying family news in both directions. Sraffa spent the summer of 1930 in the USSR visiting Giulia in a convalescence home. In August, he was joined by his Cambridge economics colleague Maurice Dobb, a Party member, and together they did a series of guided factory tours.

Sraffa never renounced his political independence, was never a card carrier. He was "a communist without a party," he said, a Marxist who hardly ever mentioned Marx, a radical who turned himself into a reserved English gent, as discreet in his public life as he was in his private life. *The Production of Commodities by Means of Commodities* is the epitome of such discretion, fascinating, as Sraffa's other Cambridge colleague, Joan Robinson, said, in "the crystalline style in which it is written." (David also remembers Joan Robinson at

CORRESPONDENCE

THE METHODS OF FASCISM.

The Case of Antonio Gramsci.

To the Editor of the Manchester Guardian.

Sir,—In view of the discussion which has been taking place in your columns on the methods of Fascism, it seems opportune to bring before your readers the facts of a recent case which can hardly be included within Mr. Shaw's category of crimes justified by "necessity."

Antonio Gramsci, a Communist deputy in the Italian Parliament and a journalist, was arrested in November, 1926, in spite of the immunity attaching to a deputy, and was banished, along with other members of the Opposition, to the Italian island of Ustica. Signor Gramsci had always been an invalid owing to a pronounced curvature of the spine, and had only been able to indulge in continuous intellectual activity—an academic study of philology at the university prior to the war and a study of Italian politics since the war—by virtue of a special regime of life and a special diet. Even the milder rigours of prison life were therefore likely to be in his case particularly serious.

A few months after his initial arrest Signor Gramsci was taken from the island and sent to Milan. This journey was by means of the extraordinarily slow and painful process by which prisoners in Italy are transferred from place to place: cramped in a small cell of a special prison coach on a crawling train all day, and breaking the journey on the way at various places—at Palermo, Reggio Calabria, Naples, Rome, Florence, Bologna,—to be housed in the dirty and vermin-infested detention cells of the local prison for days on end. In Milan he has been awaiting trial since early February. The diet of a political prisoner is usually little more than a pound of bread and soup per day. Usually this can be supplemented by gifts of food and by food bought in the canteen by money received from friends and deposited with the prison governor. In Signor Gramsci's case, however, this has not been allowed: both gifts of food and money from friends have been intercepted by the prison authorities and prevented from reaching Signor Gramsci. Friends have been prevented from seeing him, even though he has legally a perfect right to receive such visitors.

A delicate invalid from the first, Signor Gramsci has been reduced to a state of extreme emaciation by the harshness of his treatment since his arrest—treatment which would have shaken the constitution of the strongest man. Unable to digest even the meagre and poor food he receives, he is in a state of literal semi-starvation. He has several times had to be removed to the prison infirmary, and the state of his health, affecting his mouth, has caused him to lose most of his teeth in the last few weeks, so that his ability to eat the coarse prison fare is still further lessened. After nine months of such treatment this man has now to undergo a further journey to Rome to stand his trial, at which he is likely to be sentenced to a long term of imprisonment, probably twenty or thirty years, for the crime of organising opposition to the Fascist regime.—Yours, &c.,

AN ITALIAN IN ENGLAND.

Cambridge, decked out in a Chinese jacket and red star Mao cap.) Without explicitly stating it, Sraffa justified Marx's labor theory of value, that the rate of exploitation is more fundamental than the rate of profit on capital.

The Production of Commodities by Means of Commodities also quietly shredded neoclassical economic theory, pulling the rug from beneath the feet of bourgeois orthodoxy, demonstrating the tautology of its supply and demand nostrums. That the rate of profit is measured by the productivity of capital is meaningless nonsense, Sraffa said, something that sent you round in vacuous circles: you have to know the level of prices to know the value of capital, and you have to know the rate of profit to know the level of prices. Supply and demand explains nothing, grips onto nothing, fetishizes everything. Sraffa sticks to his Marxian guns, agreeing with Marx (and Ricardo) that the prices of commodities are proportional to the labor-time required to produce them. The real nub of economic theory, he said, is *value*, the rate of *exploitation* of labor.

Sraffa was brilliant at revealing how prices relate to value. He offered an ingenious solution to the "transformation problem" in Marxist theory, using algebra to work out the conversion of commodity values into market prices, calculating how the rate of exploitation is related to the rate of profit on capital, a puzzle Sraffa reckoned was more analytical than actual. The real economics of capitalism, he said, functioned precisely as the Marx of Volume 1 of *Capital* had posited it. The equations, said Sraffa, qualifying his own contribution, "show that the conditions of exchange are entirely determined by the conditions of production."

GRAMSCI AND SRAFFA FIRST ENCOUNTERED EACH OTHER in 1919, in Turin, via an intermediary, Umberto Cosmo, who'd actually taught Sraffa Italian at high school; Cosmo went on to hold a professorship at the University of Turin where Gramsci became one of his brightest literature students. When Gramsci founded the magazine *L'Ordine Nuovo* (*The New Order*) on May Day 1919, Sraffa joined its editorial team and soon their friendship thrived. Sraffa reported on economic affairs and penned several important articles on labor struggles in the United States and Britain. (His name, though, never figured as author, nor was Sraffa ever listed on the magazine's masthead.) *L'Ordine Nuovo* ran as a "weekly review of socialist culture." "Its only unifying sentiment," Gramsci said, "arose out of a vague passion for a vague proletarian culture. We wanted to act, act, act."

The magazine sought to transcend sectarianism, promote open discussion, the exchange of ideas, and actively encouraged comradely disagreement and debate. Not a Party vehicle, never slavishly following any official line, its perspective, said Gramsci, was autonomous and international. In April 1924, he and Sraffa voiced their own pointed disagreement about how to fight fascism. "From an old subscriber and friend of *L'Ordine Nuovo*," Gramsci cued Sraffa's contribution, "we've received the following letter." "I stand by my opinion," Sraffa began, "that the working class is totally absent from political life. And I can only conclude that the Communist Party, *today*, can do nothing or almost nothing positive."

Workers these days, Sraffa wrote, don't see concrete problems as political problems: they present themselves as something resolvable "individually" and "privately," as actions done purely "to preserve job, pay, house and family." As such, said Sraffa, "I don't think that a relaxation of fascist pressure can be secured by the Communist Party; today is the hour of democratic opposition, and I think it is necessary to let them proceed and even help them. What is necessary, first of all, is a bourgeois revolution, which will then allow the development of a working-class politics."

The Communist Party "commits a grave error," Sraffa said, "when it gives the impression it is sabotaging an alliance of oppositional forces"; it's "only *afterward*, after the fall of fascism, that the Party will have to distinguish itself as the party of the masses; and certainly the Southern question and unity of the working classes and peasants will be in the forefront. But not today." Its function for now, Sraffa concluded, signing off simply as "S.," "is that of a *coach-fly*"—after La Fontaine's fable, in which a group of horses dragging a heavy load up a steep hill has a fly hovering over them; the fly believes it's his own effort that makes the horses' arduous ascent successful.

In his tart response, Gramsci said "this letter contains all the necessary and sufficient elements to liquidate a revolutionary organization such as our party is and must be. And yet, this isn't the intention of our friend S., who even though he isn't a member, even though he's only on the fringes of our movement and propaganda, has faith in our party and considers it the only one capable of permanently resolving the problems posed and the situation created by fascism." Our friend S., Gramsci said, treads on dangerous ground, reducing the efficacy of a powerful oppositional force. He dissolves its impact, relegates it to another reformist entity—to another passive non-force—which was part of the problem in letting fascism grow in the first place.

"Our friend S. doesn't adopt the viewpoint of an organized party," said Gramsci. "So he doesn't perceive the consequences of his views or the numerous contradictions into which he falls." What is required is a leading light, a beacon, Gramsci said, "a role of guide and vanguard," and that's precisely what the Communist Party offers—or should offer: "an organized fraction of the proletariat and of the peasant masses, i.e. of the classes which are today oppressed and crushed by fascism.... If our party doesn't find *for today* independent solutions of its own to Italian problems, the classes which are its natural base would turn over *en masse* toward other political currents." Our friend S., in sum, "hasn't yet succeeded in destroying in himself the ideological traces of his democratic-liberal intellectual formation, normative and Kantian rather than dialectical and Marxist."

THAT STRANGE FIGURE DAVID SAW ALL THOSE DECADES ago harbored something deep: he was one of the last people to see Gramsci alive twenty years earlier. He and Gramsci met a final time at Quisisana clinic on March 25, 1937, in Rome, exactly a month and two days before Gramsci's passing. With ever declining health, Gramsci had obtained yet another transfer, ridding himself of the Formia clinic, arriving at Quisisana on August 24, 1935, where, in northern Rome, he would conclude his days—not far from where this end had begun on November 8, 1926, on that long night of his arrest. When Sraffa came in March, Gramsci knew he was due to be released later in April; he'd been considering his future, what he'd do as a free man, where he'd live. He and Sraffa discussed it.

Two options presented themselves to Gramsci: either emigrate to the USSR, rejoin his wife and sons, repair their relationship, and continue to pursue his political activities, or else return to Sardinia, retire, and try to recuperate his health in his native village. It seemed the former option was preferable to Gramsci, because Sraffa already had documentation from the Soviet authorities that would enable the process. At their meeting, Gramsci said he also had an important message he wanted his friend to convey to the PCI leadership in Paris, a piece of advice, a recommendation about its strategy, about what it should do to confront fascism.

Gramsci's position had now taken a new turn, evolving since his disagreement with Sraffa a decade or so prior. No longer did he believe there could be a direct passage from fascism to socialism. Some interim position, a tactical transitional phase would be necessary, and here the only realistic option, he said, was to develop a "Constituent Assembly," an alliance between the PCI and other anti-fascist parties. Thus his message to the PCI: "The Popular Front in Italy is the Constituent Assembly." *Nota bene*.

The record indicates that, as ever, Sraffa was loyal to his friend. He immediately communicated Gramsci's message to Togliatti, through the intermediary Mario Montagnana, Togliatti's brother-in-law, a member of the PCI Central Committee in Paris. Years later, in a letter dated December 18, 1969, addressed to the labor historian Paolo Spriano, Sraffa declared: "I remember with certainty one of the last times I visited him at the Quisisana in Rome, Gramsci asked me to transmit his urgent recommendation that the policy position of the Constituent Assembly be adopted; I reported this in Paris."

What did Party bigwigs make of Gramsci's recommendation? It's hard to tell. Negatively, likely, incredulously, probably; maybe Gramsci was proposing something that further isolated him from Togliatti et al., from those men at the top? Was it a volte-face by the Party's co-founder? Had the fascists softened him, eventually destroyed his brain, finally stopped it from working? Or had his terrible ordeal and sufferings made him acutely aware of the gravity of the situation—one of which the Party's cushy leadership, safe and sound in a distant city, had little real inkling? Maybe Gramsci's affirmation of a Constituent Assembly mimicked the pragmatism of the Soviet New Economic Policy (NEP), when, in 1922, Lenin insisted on a little dose of free market capitalism to help stimulate the ailing Communist economy, allowing state enterprises to operate on a profit basis.

Or maybe it was simply Gramsci's savvy *realpolitik*, a leaf out of the playbook of his hero, Machiavelli. Now, the most efficacious immediate strategy of Gramsci's party, of the *Modern Prince*—which, remember, was no longer a superior individual leader but the popular masses wedded to the Party—is that of the wily fox not the roaring lion. Thirteen years on, Gramsci knew all too well the traps and snares out to ambush the lion, understood them because he'd fallen for them. Now, he recognized that the struggle for post-fascist hegemony required a period of consent, of incorporation and inclusiveness—not of direct oppositional assault. Had Sraffa been right all along?

On the other hand, maybe this just harked back to the so-called dual perspective, something Gramsci had outlined in Notebook 13 on Machiavelli, discussing it with his fellow inmates at Turi prison as early as 1930. It was really all about the ebb and flow of political action, the vicissitudes and vagaries of doing politics, where force and consent, fortune and virtue change, blow in the wind, and any Modern Prince needed to anticipate in which direction it breezed. After fascism's demise, and prior to the proletariat seizing power, Gramsci thought there would likely be an intervening, transitional period; the Party should take this into account. He didn't see any absolute separation between the moment of consent and the moment of force, between reform and revolution. It wasn't about two forms of "immediacy," Gramsci said, "which succeed each other mechanically in time." Rather, the two coexist and represent two ways of fighting, provided they're dialectically conjoined.

The important thing, Gramsci said, "is seeing them clearly: in other words, accurately identifying the fundamental and permanent elements of the process." He again illustrates the point through Machiavelli, his favored man of thought and action, a partisan and creator, "an initiator" who spoke to Gramsci "in the future tense" (as Althusser said)—Italy's first Jacobin.

"Machiavelli neither creates from nothing," Gramsci said, "nor does he move in the turbid void of his own desires and dreams. He bases himself on *effective reality*" (emphasis added). And so, perhaps, now, in 1937, near the end of his life, offering it as a sort of last political will and testament, Gramsci recognized that the most effective reality was the "Constituent Assembly," something politically "conjunctual" rather than "organic." The Modern Prince, Gramsci knew, just as the old Prince of Machiavelli knew, that in politics you're judged by only one criterion: *success*.

INTERESTINGLY, A FELLOW INMATE OF GRAMSCI'S AT TURI prison, another political prisoner, was a former railway worker and Party member called Athos Lisa. Lisa (born 1890) was almost an exact contemporary of Gramsci's and remembers the two-week stint of morning lectures Gramsci gave prisoners in the autumn of 1930. Lisa's "Report" on Gramsci's political views in prison formed part of a memoir, kept secret in Lisa's lifetime, and was only discovered by his widow after Lisa's death in 1965, tucked away in the bottom of his desk drawer. (An English translation of this "Report" appears as an "Annexe" to Perry Anderson's book version of *The Antinomies of Antonio Gramsci*.)

Lisa's "Report" claimed Togliatti concealed Gramsci's message about the Constituent Assembly, passed on by Sraffa, because the PCI was peddling its own illusions that a socialist revolution was just around the corner, and that the Party was the only opposition to fascism. Togliatti, in other words, rejected Gramsci's views because of political power plays. Lisa made it clear that, for Gramsci, the Constituent Assembly wasn't a permanent state of PCI, being only a temporary waystation toward a more distant goal, and this goal remained steadfastly Communist, an affirmation rather than dilution of Gramsci's militant politics.

He was still fully committed to overthrowing the capitalist state, through military organization, through revolution. The Party needed to create hegemony in the classic Leninist sense, laying the groundwork for its "war of position," developing the conditions for the decisive moment of struggle when heavy hammer blows could be inflicted on the bourgeois state apparatus, shattering it irrevocably; and a new form of government would succeed it, a socialist state—an "integral state," Machiavelli had called it.

Under Togliatti's watch, the PCI buried Gramsci's view not because of its reformism but because of its revolutionary thrust, going much further to the left than anything the Party was really envisaging, notwithstanding its anti-capitalist bluster. For that reason, said Lisa, Gramsci announced his lecture series as "a punch in the eye" to the PCI's official line. What's more, after the fall of fascism, Gramsci said that Italy must purge itself of its reactionary past, that every fascist minister should be banished from the state apparatus, for good, excluded from ever practicing government anywhere, in any capacity, at all times.

As history had it, in 1946 a Constituent Assembly became political reality in Italy, took over the helm of government, yet with a bitter twist—with a punch in the eye, if you will, to Gramsci. To be sure, almost every politician and prefect who'd served under Mussolini remained in office somewhere, and their careers prospered, including Enrico Macis, the infamous Judge of the Special Tribunal who'd sentenced Gramsci to his slow prison death. (Between 1927 and 1943, this Special Tribunal had passed over 4,500 sentences, totaling around 28,000 years of imprisonment, including 42 death sentences, of which 31 were fulfilled.) And, incidentally, in that same government was Gramsci's former PCI running mate, Palmiro Togliatti, who became Minister of Justice. The PCI's rightward drift was assured, had commenced early, silently and unabatedly, and would continue its slide until eventual dissolution on February 3, 1991.

As for Sraffa himself, in the 1960s the PCI tried to lure the retired Trinity College lecturer back to Italy, wanting to appoint him Honorary President of the Gramsci Institute in Rome, but he turned the offer down. The PCI had another go in 1975, through the auspices of Georgio Napolitano, and yet again, like Joyce had Stephen Dedalus say in *Ulysses*, responding to a similar kind invitation, "promptly, inexplicably, with amicability, gratefully it was declined."

"DEAR FRIEND," TATIANA WROTE SRAFFA ON MAY 12, 1937, "I waited so long to answer and to describe our great misfortune in detail . . . I want you to write to me whether you think it useful, or, rather, absolutely necessary, that you put Nino's manuscripts in order. I thought it best to put off sending anything in order to find out whether you are willing to take charge of, and revise, this material, with the help of one of us in the family."

"The cremation has already taken place," Tatiana told Sraffa, almost matter-of-factly. "Nino suffered a cerebral hemorrhage the evening of April twenty-fifth." That day, she said, he seemed his usual self, maybe even more serene than he had been of late. He ate his dinner—soup with pasta, a fruit compote, and a bit of sponge cake. Then he left to go to the bathroom. But he was brought back in a chair, carried by several clinic nursing staff. He'd had a seizure, lost control of the whole of his left side, and collapsed on the floor, managing to crawl to the bathroom door to cry out for help. He was put back into bed and attended to by assorted doctors.

Nino lost all sensitivity and mobility on his left side, Tatiana said, and became very weary. The doctors applied leeches to bleed him, yet he started vomiting and breathing with difficulty.

The patient's condition, doctors said, was "extremely grave." "I was forced to protest violently against the priest and sisters who came in," Tatiana told Sraffa, "so they'd leave Antonio alone." Then he seemed to settle and breathe more easily. "But twenty-four hours after the attack," Tatiana said, "the violent vomiting began again, and his breathing became terribly painful." "I kept watch over him all the time. But he took a last deep breath and sunk into a silence that never could change." The doctor confirmed Tatiana's deepest fears, that he was gone, that it was all over, at 4:10 a.m. on April twenty-seventh; the sisters came to carry his diminutive body to the mortuary chamber.

Rome's police chief issued the following notice that same day: *"I report that the transportation of the body known as Antonio Gramsci, accompanied only by relatives, took place this evening at 19:30. The hearse proceeded at a trot from the clinic to the Verano cemetery where the body was deposited to await cremation."*

"Carlo and I were the only persons present," Tatiana said in her letter to Sraffa, "except for the numerous police guards who followed the body out and watched the cremation. Now the ashes have been deposited in a zinc box, laid inside a wooden one and set in a place reserved by the government... I will request authorization to transport it."

TATIANA MIRACULOUSLY SMUGGLED GRAMSCI'S MANU-scripts out of the Quisisana clinic, lord knows how, and Sraffa's friend, Raffaele Mattioli, Managing Director of the Banca Commerciale Italia, helped her use a safe deposit box at the bank's Rome head office to preserve the notebooks, keeping them out of the dirty maulers of the fascist authorities. Later, they were mailed to the USSR, arriving in Moscow in July 1938, a little more than a year after Gramsci's death. At the Quisisana clinic, a memorial plaque was put up in the deceased Communist's honor, yet has since been removed: the clinic's owner, Giuseppe Ciarrapico, who died in 2019, age eighty-five, had requested it in his will. In recent times, the plot has thickened and now left and right tussle on the legacy of Gramsci at Quisisana.

Ciarrapico was a former senator in Silvio Berlusconi's *Popolo delle Libertà* (The People of Freedom) Party, a redoubtable fascist and multimillionaire embezzler, convicted several times for financial misdemeanors, helping himself in the early 2000s to 20 million euros of public monies. Along with an array of health clinics (like the Quisisana), Ciarrapico owned bottled water plants, restaurants, air-taxi services, publishing houses and newspapers, and was president and owner of AS Roma football club, which he'd acquired in 1991. A nasty character, of a nasty family, who still own Quisisana.

In December 2023, the cold case of getting a plaque installed at Gramsci's death site reopened. After a presentation of the agenda at the Rome city council, incumbent Democratic Party (PD) mayor Roberto Gualtieri said he was committed to the proposed plaque, born out of a petition organized by the leftist newspaper *Il Manifesto*, with over 2,500 signatories. The Quisisana clinic confirmed it was "largely satisfied" with the favorable vote for affixing a commemoration, likely something erected on the inside rather than on the outside. "The vote," commented the first signatory, Erica Battaglia (PD), "allows for a faster and more inclusive process to give just memory to one of the most important political and philosophical thinkers of the twentieth century."

After I returned to Italy from New York, I was curious if there'd been any activity at Quisisana, any hint that a plaque might go up somewhere soon. And so off I went again on another little Gramsci adventure, visiting another site of his buried past, riding a Lime rental bike the four miles or so from my Monti home, journeying beyond Villa Borghese, to the clinic that today is known as Casa di Cura di Quisisana, in the smart bougie neighborhood of Parioli.

Along Via Gran Giacomo Porro, Casa di Cura di Quisisana is plush with its marble-pillared rotunda entrance. Flanked by luscious palm trees, it looks more like the glitzy casino at Monte Carlo than any healthcare institution; the mind boggles comparing it with what the British National Health Service (NHS) could ever serve up. The security guard at the reception paid me no attention as I waltzed in, faking authority, looking like I knew where I was, where I was headed, and I ventured toward the clinic's pleasant little café, with bright sunshine flooding through its windowed back wall. I ordered an obligatory espresso, which I

drank, as you do, in a couple of gulps standing at the bar. Then I sat down, surveyed the surroundings, looking at the crucifixes adorning the walls, at the well-heeled people coming and going. I have no idea whether the clinic was as upscale in Gramsci's day, whose costs were borne by Sraffa. What I do know is that Gramsci was under constant police surveillance here and never left the premises.

On one wall I noticed a framed photograph showing Quisisana under construction, with its scaffolding gaping, and I couldn't help noticing the date—1926—ironically the year of Gramsci's arrest. As I sat there, I held my own private communion: I was tremendously moved by the thought that, here, eighty-seven years ago, Gramsci died, in this very building, and I was sitting in it, in Rome, now, on a Friday afternoon in April, a beautiful warm sunny day, thinking wouldn't it be nice to see a large mural of Gramsci in the café on one of its walls, maybe an image of him in his youth, looking vibrant and a little dash, with a simple inscription below—I don't know, maybe something like, *è qui che morti Gramsci*. It was here where Gramsci died. Wishful thinking, perhaps, because we'll have to wait and see what transpires, what the Rome city council's motion might eventually bring forth, and what the rightist Ciarrapico family accepts in its private fiefdom . . .

7

DEAD AND ALIVE

The final week in April is a biggie in the Gramsci calendar at Rome's Non-Catholic cemetery. The 25th is "Liberation Day," a national holiday here in Italy, commemorating the victory of the nation's Resistance movement against Nazi Germany and the Italian fascist state; and two days later, on the 27th, is the commemoration of Gramsci's death at the hands of the said fascist regime. Liberation Day has obvious attraction for Gramscians. Alas, the event itself came too late for the man, toasted eight years after his demise. Yet he's remembered, honored on this day, as an inspiring icon in the victory over fascism. That his brain continues to function—on the page, in dozens of languages, across cultures, in people's lives—immortalizes him as one of fascism's greatest failures.

The 25th of April saw Gramsci admirers and well-wishers appear in droves, showing up nonstop throughout the morning, between nine and 1 p.m., from the cemetery's opening until its half-day closing. Before long, Gramsci's grave was aglow with flowers and bouquets, and volunteers from the Fondazione Gramsci held an early morning vigil. A group of twenty or so people, mainly elderly women, paid homage, some lovingly tending the flowers around the tombstone and casket, doing so as if they were communing with a dearly departed loved one, a deceased husband or father, meticulously arranging everything, clearing away the dust and debris from Gramsci's little patch. And then there was a moving reading, a middle-aged man reciting one of Gramsci's well-known letters to his younger brother, Carlo (December 19, 1929):

> It seems to me that under such conditions prolonged for years, and with such psychological experiences, a man should have reached the loftiest stage of stoic serenity and should have acquired such a profound conviction that man bears within himself the source of his own moral strength, that everything depends on him, on his energy, on his will, on the iron coherence of the aims that he sets for himself and the means he adopts to realize them, that he will never again despair or lapse into those vulgar, banal states of the mind that are called pessimism and optimism. My state of mind synthesizes these two emotions and overcomes them: I'm a pessimist because of intelligence, but an optimist of the will.

Later in the morning, a much younger bunch arrived, eighteen masters' students from the Erasmus University Rotterdam in the Netherlands, wanting to see Gramsci, a multinational crew hailing from all over the world, from Ireland and Colombia, from the Lebanon and Switzerland, from France and Germany, from Spain and the UK. Ordinarily, a group of this size would have to book in advance to gain entry; but on this special day an exception was made, and I was asked by the Visitor's Office to lead them to Gramsci's grave, to supervise them a bit. Standing before Gramsci, beside his floral tribute, I couldn't help chipping

in a few words of my own, about his being at the Non-Catholic
Cemetery, about how it all came to be, and about the significance
of today for Gramscians.

Then I asked, *Why Gramsci?* What did he mean to them,
twentysomething graduate students in Public Policy, to which
Sinead, from Ireland, answered that he corrected several things
Marx got wrong, or else understated—about culture and ideology,
about the importance of things that weren't just economic, but
were superstructural, and no less important for that. Another said
his anti-dogmatism had universal appeal, that he spoke to their
generation, went across generations. "Look, we're here, right,"
somebody said. "That alone is testimony, isn't it?"—testimony
to his enduring appeal, to young and old progressives—though
perhaps not quite alike.

The encounters on the 25th were smaller dress rehearsals for
the main event on April 27: the commemoration of the main man,
a commemoration that was also a celebration of his living on, of
his still breathing life, inspiring in us moral strength, reminding
us, in case we forget, that together we bear within ourselves our
own destiny, that everything depends on us, on our energy and
on our will, on our iron coherence of the aims we set ourselves.
Gramsci famously transcends optimism and pessimism, overcomes them, keeps hope alive: for us he is both dead and alive,
the dialectical incarnation of commemoration and celebration, of
the past and the future, of our grieving his life yet thriving off his
thought, off his example.

Hence the significance of April 27—indeed so significant in
the cemetery's activities that it warranted a very special act: the
opening of "*La Porta di Gramsci*," "Gramsci's Gate," a large
pair of heavy iron gates along Via Nicola Zabaglia, which, when
pulled apart, offer immediate access to Gramsci's tomb. (The
door's key fob is marked "Gramsci's Gate.") With these doors

open, cemetery volunteers, including yours truly, had to stand guard, turning away any non-Gramscians. We needed to be on the lookout for potential fascist disruptors, too, while steering regular visitors toward the main entrance around the corner on Via Caio Cestio. Those in the know come to the side gate, come every year, to celebrations organized by Rome's Fondazione Gramsci and the Italian branch of the International Gramsci Society, headquartered in the United States.

Point to note: the two groups don't get along, don't talk to one another, are at odds with each other; and on the morning of the 27th they conduct their own separate ceremonies. It's a sectarian tiff, seemingly baseless for the uninitiated, baseless even for the initiated. The Fondazione Gramsci accuse the International Gramsci Society of being *traditori*—traitors. For what reason?

It's hard to know. When I heard the likes, it reminded me of Nikolai Gogol's short story "The Quarrel of the Two Ivans," about two dear friends who fall out. Once, the two Ivans were inseparable, so close that they loved each other like brothers, living in houses next to each other in a little Ukrainian village, sharing meals together, united by much more than mere name— until, until . . . one day they have a nonsensical tiff about a rifle and one Ivan calls the other Ivan "a goose"—"*How dare you, in disregard of all decency, call me a goose.*"

And that's that, the collapse of a beautiful friendship, like calling someone a Stalinist or Trotskyist, a revisionist or Hegelian, even a "traitor." Gogol ends his short story on a depressing note, that our world is "rather gloomy, gentlemen," when friends with more similarities than differences can't get along—didn't Freud call it "the narcissism of minor difference"?

One wonders what Gramsci himself might have made of the squabble between the two Ivans, between the Fondazione Gramsci and the International Gramsci Society, between two groups who speak in his name, who operate in his honor, who keep his thought and legacy alive, and yet who can't get along, overcome their grievances. Is it really respecting Gramsci's legacy? Didn't Gramsci have the ability to unite warring, ideologically divided factions? Wouldn't he have been dismayed, particularly later in his life, at such sectarian mentality?

At ten-thirty, the Fondazione Gramsci unveiled a large wreath of crimson roses, adorned with their organization's banner, and fifty or so people, most on the older side of the age spectrum, gathered around Gramsci in hushed reverence. Sometimes it seemed more like embarrassing silence, like waiting for Godot, expectant of something that didn't look like happening. Eventually, something did happen, someone read aloud an extract of Pasolini's poem "*Le ceneri di Gramsci*," "Gramsci's Ashes":

And you, here, banished with your hard, uncatholic grace,
registered among the dead foreigners: Gramsci's ashes. . . .Torn
between hope and disillusion . . . the darkness of the foreign
garden, you are dead and we are likewise dead with you, in this
humid garden. Only here, you see, on foreign ground, may you
rest, still an outcast.

The meeting of the International Gramsci Society at midday
was livelier, a more numerous affair: a hundred and fifty people
of varying ages, including a lot of younger folk, congregated with
a red rose in hand. It was a badge of entry at Gramsci's Gate,
a lovely gesture, especially when we think of the significance of
roses for Gramsci, the cultivator of flowers, nurturing his little

garden, his tiny plot along Turi prison's wall, as if he were trying to establish his own mini-utopia, full of beauty yet something durable, with a capacity to survive all weathers and occasionally to pique with its thorns.

Onlookers heard speeches and readings of Gramsci's letters to his mother:

Dearest Mamma . . . I can't give you many details about the accusations against me, since up to now I haven't been able to understand exactly what they are. In any case, the issue is clearly political . . . One simply has to have a great deal of patience. I have a ton of it, wagonfuls, whole housefuls. Do you remember what Carlo used to say when he was little and had eaten some special dessert?—"I want a hundred housefuls

of it!"... But you, too, must be good and patient. Your letter
shows me that you are quite the opposite. You write that you
feel old, etc. Well, I'm sure that you're still very strong and
resilient despite your age, the sorrows you have known, and
the great efforts that you had to make. (February 26, 1927)

Dearest Mamma ... I no longer know what to write to comfort
you and set your mind at peace.... I'm neither a child nor
simpleton, don't you agree? My life has always been ruled and
directed by my convictions, which certainly were never passing
whims nor momentary improvisations. (December 12, 1927)

Dearest Mamma ... Prison is a very ugly thing; but for me
dishonor due to moral weakness and cowardice would be even

worse. So you mustn't be alarmed and grieve too much, and you must never think that I'm downcast and desperate. You must have patience and in any case you mustn't believe the nonsense they publish about me. (March 12, 1928)

Dearest Mamma, I would really like to embrace you and hold you tight to make you feel how much I love you and how I would like to console you for this sorrow that I've caused you: but I couldn't have acted otherwise. Life is like that, very hard, and sometimes sons must be the cause of great sorrow for their mothers if they wish to preserve their honor and their dignity as men. I embrace you tenderly, Nino. (May 10, 1928)

Someone else spoke about having just returned from Latin America, and about how many young people over there were inspired by Gramsci's life and writings, how it was thrilling to see his thought speak to those of different tongues and cultures, retaining its significance across time and space—Gramsci was a true internationalist, he said, and in that sense it struck me then that Pasolini's poem got Gramsci wrong, objecting to his being put to rest among "foreigners."

I've got to admit I'm not too keen on Pasolini's tribute to Gramsci: too downbeat for me, too chauvinistically Italian, wanting to narrow Gramsci's breadth of appeal, reclaiming him as an Italian fit only for Italian soil, buried exclusively among Italians. He was a Sardinian-Italian Internationalist married to a Russian. *"On foreign ground, you're still an outcast,"* Pasolini says, without seeing how inclusively global he was, and how inclusively global he continues to be.

Then a journalist from the leftist newspaper *Il Manifesto* made his way forward and began discussing the campaign to get a commemorative plaque at the Quisisana clinic. He reminded everybody that, on this very day, Gramsci died in northern Rome, about six miles up the road, and there's still no memorial for him there. He mentioned the petition, still ongoing, trying to accumulate signatories, and the fact that there needed to be popular pressure on the municipality and on the clinic, which, he said, confirming something I knew already, is a privately owned establishment, controlled by a family with deep fascist sympathies; we should organize around getting Gramsci memorialized as Quisisana. To which everyone clapped.

By morning's end, Gramsci was blooming with flowers. The single rose I saw on his casket several months earlier had now propagated into something vaster, into a whole rose movement, into a plurality of roses, a great floral remembrance, a

stunning reminder that, yes, Gramsci was right, might always
be right: flowers will outlast weeds and today I'd just witnessed
my *Roses for Gramsci—smelled* them, watched them grow into
something fecund and meaningful. I forgot about any comradely
disagreement.

As I stood guard at Gramsci's Gate, keeping an eye out for
those who came and went, I was really more a spectator than a
participant, a fly on the Aurelian wall. But this gave me the mental
space to reflect upon what I was witnessing, what was bringing
these people together—what did they see in Gramsci, and who
were they? Maybe what Gramsci brings to the table, to their
table, is his special notion of intellectuals, a breed of people who
have the capacity to think and struggle for a better society.

I don't mean this rhetorically; it's a more modest, everyday
understanding, of making justice ordinary, of bringing Marxism
closer to home, of embedding it in the context of real people's
lives, of ordinary people united by their capacity to think. They
were all intellectuals in the Gramscian sense of the term. Everyone
is an intellectual, Gramsci says, but not all in society have the
function of intellectuals. "Each person," he says, "outside of their
professional activity, carries on some form of intellectual activity,
they are 'philosophers,' an artist, somebody of taste, they partici-
pate in a particular conception of the world, have a conscious line
of moral conduct, and therefore contribute to sustain a conception of the world or to modify it, to bring into being new modes
of thought."

I suspect this describes a lot of the people who showed up on
April 25 and 27: they hold a particular conception of the world
and, drawing from Gramsci, a conscious line of moral conduct
that tries to ward off reactionary conceptions of the world. In their
own everyday lives, they're likely "permanent persuaders," some
sort of organizer or instructor or teacher, maybe not teachers in

the formal sense of an occupation; rather they're political animals involved in the dissemination of modes of behavior and codes of conduct. They distinguish themselves, as Gramsci says, "less by their profession than by their function in directing the ideas and aspirations of the class to which they belong," a class that somehow speaks in the name of the working class.

Likely the aspect defining these "neo-organic intellectuals"—those Gramscians without a discernible party—is that they're all involved in the transmission and absorption of critical ideas, all, somewhere and somehow, involved in a struggle for an anti-capitalist life. They're all trying to make an ordinary life a little less ordinary, and Gramsci is their guiding spirit, somebody worth following, a moral compass, a symbol of resistance and dissent. At some point in their lives they've probably also asked themselves the probing Gramscian question: "What is man?"—or *"What is a person?"*

Likely, too, they've accepted his response, used it to enlighten their lives. "When we ask, 'what is a person?'" Gramsci says, "we really mean, 'what can a person become?', whether or not a person can control their own destiny, can 'make themselves,' can create a life for themselves. Therefore we say that a person is a process, and precisely the process of their actions. When we consider it, the question 'What is a person?' isn't an abstract or 'objective' question. It stems from what we have thought about ourselves and others, and, relative to what we have thought and seen, we seek to know what we are and what we can become… We want to know this 'now,' in the given conditions of the present and of our 'daily' life."

It's a form of self-inquiry undertaken by intelligent people. What's crucial, Gramsci says, is to conceive a person, and to conceive of oneself, as "a series of active relationships," as "an ensemble of relationships." "Individuality, while of the greatest importance," he says, "isn't the sole element to be considered." "Personality is the whole mass of relationships," and "the acquiring of a personality means acquiring a consciousness of these relationships." The inquiring person, in short, knows that there's a reality beyond the self, that we belong to a society with others, constituted by others, by ourselves with others.

THERE'S PLENTY THAT STRIKES ONE ABOUT THE GRAMSCI oeuvre, but one thing is perhaps unique: it inspires a body of thought as well as *the inspiration of the man himself*. Gramsci wasn't an ogre or despot, an autocrat or dogmatist, wasn't a towering leader or alpha male. He was a victim without ever wallowing in victimhood. He never wanted anybody to shed him any tears. His stoicism and patience warrants admiration. He was an underdog, an invalided subaltern, concerned about the state of his underwear and fussing over how he could find the right needle to darn his socks. This is what makes him so approachable, reveals his human face, a frailty and humility—remember his first apologetic prison letter to landlady Clara Passarge? Such humble qualities seemed to attract women followers, explaining why the majority of people gathering around Gramsci on the 25th and 27th were in fact women, not just elderly women, but younger women, too. Women comprise a sizeable contingent of his fan base, always did.

Indeed, Gramsci's whole life was populated by women; he was surrounded by them—by his wife and sister-in-law, by his sisters and landlady, by his mother. Everywhere women were the protagonists in his life. (Sraffa was the sole male persona, his only man friend of any significance.) Even today, most days, it is women from the Fondazione Gramsci who come to tend his grave, who place fresh flowers on it, who dispense with old ones, and who tidy up the soil and wipe off the dust. It's done with the same tireless dedication of Tatiana's long ago, and it's a loyalty that continues, never ceases to tire.

The single most dominant woman for Gramsci was, of course, his mother, Giuseppina ("Peppinna") Marcias Gramsci, a native Sardinian, who raised Nino and his six siblings almost single-handedly, often with little help from husband Francesco, a man of Albanian descent. Francesco was employed in the Land Registry Office of Sorgono, a neighboring village; but between 1898 and 1904 he was imprisoned for the misuse of public funds, for "financial irregularities." After his release, work was scant and money scarce for the Gramscis. Giuseppina was the daughter of a local tax collector, better educated and more cultivated than a lot of other Ghilarza housewives. But Francesco's jailtime meant financial hardship and not a little humiliation for Gramsci's mother.

She wasn't forgotten on the day of her son's anniversary. As events unfolded in Rome, a similar ceremony took place in Ghilarza's small public cemetery. The newspaper *L'unione Sarda* reported on a "touching and simple floral tribute to his mother's tomb on the 87th anniversary of Antonio Gramsci's death." A handful of people congregated, and a wreath was laid down by Galatea Gramsci, "the niece of the thinker, who read out a letter from prison written to Gramsci's mother." The commemoration was organized by Ghilarza's Casa Museo Antonio Gramsci, whose president, Catherina Pes, spoke about the ongoing building works undertaken at the museum, the site of Gramsci's childhood home. She explained what the museum is doing to preserve Gramsci's legacy. "The works are slightly late," she admitted, but we're reassured that "by July [2024] the renovations will be completed, and we will make the structure accessible to everyone again." For the time being, Pes said, "part of the collection can be admired in the nearby premises of Piazza Gramsci."

The most poignant of all Gramsci's letters to his mother was dated March 8, 1934: "I don't know much about your health," Gramsci says. "Teresina writes little and the same goes for Grazietta. I hope from now on to write regularly, even though not too often. Dearest Mother, I embrace you with all my affection, together with everyone at home." We know she never read this letter. We know it because his mother had already been dead for fifteen months, passing away on December 30, 1932. But nobody had the heart to tell Nino. Tatiana said they were reluctant for fear of pushing him over the edge, that he'd be unable to withstand the shock; it would propel him down the abyss he'd been staring down. Tatiana said his physical and mental health had deteriorated over the past year and a half to such a degree that he no longer had the strength even to write regular letters; since 1933, his correspondence had noticeably trailed off. All of which begs the question: Did Gramsci ever find out the truth? Did he ever know his mother was dead?

What is evident is that his final months were mysterious, not least concerning what he'd do after April 21, 1937, once freed. Sraffa's testimony hinted at expatriation to the USSR, being reunited with his family, continuing the communist struggle. A clearcut decision, no? But then, suddenly, a change of plan, opting instead to return to Sardinia. Why? In the early 2000s, Antonio Gramsci Jr., Gramsci's grandson, Giuliano's son, intrigued, undertook his own investigation into the matter. He looked into the history of the Schucht family and tried to reconstruct the life of his grandfather around its conclusion. (In 2012, Gramsci Jr. presented his thesis to an audience at Turin's Teatro Vittoria. The talk was translated into English and published as "My Grandfather" in the November/December 2016 issue of *New Left Review*.)

The Schuchts, Gramsci Jr. says, were long-standing friends with the Ulyanovs, Lenin's family. *The Register of Biographical Records of Lenin* reveals that Gramsci met the Bolshevik leader at the Kremlin on October 25, 1922, and the two men, despite more than a twenty-year age gap, got along. Lenin was impressed with the young Italian. He favored him as the head of the Italian Communist Party, in preference to Amadeo Bordiga, who disappointed Lenin with his sectarian rigidity. The record says that Lenin and Gramsci spoke about Italy's "southern question," about the state of the Italian Socialist Party, and its possible fusion with the Communists. Yet after Lenin's death, in January 1924, things under Stalin turned sourer, more suspicious.

Delving into the Russian State Archives, Gramsci Jr. discovered a complex picture of his grandfather's relationship with the Soviet security service, the NKVD. In 1936, they wanted Gramsci to tell them everything he knew about the Italian Trotskyists. Gramsci Jr. suggests that Gramsci Sr. might have balked at the prospect. That his emigration might be conditional on him collaborating with the Soviet secret service was troubling. Or, as Gramsci Jr. wonders, "Did they simply wish to make him aware, indirectly, that he still carried the taint of Trotskyist sympathies, having written a letter in defense of Trotsky to the Central Committee of the CPSU in October 1926?"

Was it at this moment, then, Gramsci Jr. muses, that his grandfather wrote to his family "begging them urgently to find him a room in Santu Lussurgiu"? Was it his worsening health, coupled with the worsening political climate in the Soviet Union, that hastened the dramatic change of course, having him select retirement on his native island? And what a hero's return it was meant to be, scheduled for April 27, 1937. Niece Edmea, daughter of eldest brother Gennaro, had found her uncle a very nice room in the village where Gramsci passed his junior high school days; and the family was naturally over the moon, thrilled about his imminent return, like Odysseus's epic homecoming to Ithaca. Gramsci's father, Francesco, then in his seventy-ninth year, was especially ecstatic about being reunited with his long-lost son, not seen since 1924, an absence of thirteen hard years.

On the morning of the 27th there was great hoo-hah and anticipation, tremendous expectation in the Gramsci household. But by evening when Nino failed to show, everybody wondered what had happened, why the delay, why no word about his arrival? They didn't know until the next day the awful truth, listening to a radio broadcast, that he'd died in Rome the day before, on the fated day of his return. Francesco, devastated, screamed, *"Assassins, murderers, they've killed my boy, killed my boy!"* It was too much to endure. Two weeks later, on May 16, 1937, Francesco himself was gone, passing away of a broken heart; the Gramsci family tragedy was complete.

Seven decades on, Gramsci's youngest son, Giuliano, began his own inquiry, a very personal one, into his father's legacy, and into his own legacy with his father. *What could he say to a father he'd never seen?* The question formed the basis of a book, *Papà Gramsci,* created in dialogue with the Italian lawyer and writer Anna Maria Sgarbi—a series of twenty imaginary letters an octogenarian Giuliano, a retired music professor from Moscow's Music Conservatory, a man who'd always preferred music to politics, finally wrote to his

late departed father: "Dear Papa, I've aged, am eighty years old. You are always the same—young, intelligent, sharp, and handsome. I've never touched you with my hands, but always caressed you on paper and embraced you in my dreams."

Giuliano's letters are emotionally charged, his heart laid bare to his father; some of the contents, Giuliano knew, would have upset Papa, and it's a good thing he never knew—it would have only added to the dreadful sufferings already inflicted upon him. *"Dear Papa,"* he begins,

> my infancy, my childhood and adolescence passed without
> freedom, with a fear of everything. . . . You know, Papa, when
> I finished first in class I received a book as a gift from school,
> with a cover of leather, titled 'Thank you, comrade Stalin, for all
> our happy childhoods.' It told of Stalin's heroic deeds, from his
> youth to these days, and also contained poems, not so beautiful.
> I remember one by the poet Stalsky, and this is what it said:

In the cloudy sky
above the snow-capped peaks
eagles fly
and the first eagle is
Lenin,
the second is
Stalin,
and eaglets,
their children
and pupils,
fly around.

The day I received the gift book at school, I went home happy and proud because it was a reward for good academic performance. Mamma dampened my enthusiasm, taking the book from me and putting it aside, without even leafing through it. I missed you very much at that moment.

Dear Papa, when Delio died in 1982, I had a real deep feeling of loneliness. . . . He was in great pain waiting for the title of admiral and was sent into retirement. He wanted promotion more than anything in the world, and when he was forced to retire before reaching this milestone, he fell ill with a severe depression that led to his death. . . . His body was placed in the tomb of Grandpa [Apollo] Schucht, where mother already rested. She died due to her illness in 1970. I remember Mother, with her grace and elegance, her wonderful violin playing, in the nursing home for old Bolsheviks in Peredelkino near Moscow. I couldn't do much for her—her illness devoured her . . .

Every now and then, when I looked at Delio, you came to mind. Delio loved to dance foxtrots and tangos, he danced everywhere; music was moving for him—joy, passion, abandonment. For me it is Bach and Vivaldi . . . I would have loved for him to speak to me as a brother, tell me his anxieties and desires, his disappointments. He left without leaving signs of weakness, and just before closing his eyes forever, he wanted to wear your glasses, because he often said that your glasses were the ones worn by all the intellectuals, the cultured people. Chekhov also wore glasses like yours, the ones without a frame, with narrow lenses perched on the nose. A hug, Giuliano.

Just before *Papà Gramsci* was released, Gramsci's youngest son wrote a taster article on the seventieth anniversary of his father's death. "Mio Padre Gramsci" appeared in the Italian national newspaper *Corriere della sera* (April 27, 2007) four months prior to Giuliano's own passing in Moscow, at the age of eighty-one. (As such, *Papà Gramsci* is even more poignant because of its posthumous publication.) In "Mio Padre Gramsci," Giuliano maintained two things: first, his father has been dispatched to "the museum of antiquity," now pretty much a forgotten man in Italy; and, second, "had he survived the atrocities of prison and found refuge in Soviet Russia, he wouldn't have had an easy time under Stalin's regime, and almost certainly would have perished in some Gulag in Siberia."

The life and death of Antonio Gramsci, we might say, was stuck between the rock and the hard place; but Giuliano was wrong about Dad: he's remembered, not forgotten, he's still an inspiration for everyone; I'd seen it for myself, seen how he's someone who still helps us navigate the rocks and hard places that besiege us everywhere today. And so, on the 27th, after everyone had left the cemetery, I closed Gramsci's great iron gate for the morning, heard it creak and clang shut, locking it, knowing he was safe for another day. Alone, in the stillness, I was able to admire the gorgeous display of flowers and wreaths next to him, the well-wisher notes and kind words. No, he's not forgotten, I reassured myself; no, he's not forgotten, I can reassure Giuliano in his far-off resting place.

Then I remembered what Gramsci said in one of his last letters to Giulia (July 1936), when he was still mulling over his future prospects. "I don't know what to do," he said, still unsure, telling his wife: "it seems to me that if I go back to Sardinia, a whole cycle of my life perhaps will be definitively closed." There and then I realized I had to go to Sardinia soon, had to go to discover it with my own eyes, had to feel the place, had to find out where Gramsci came from, and where he was about to go back to. I had to try to comprehend *what might have been*. I had to try to square that circle, understand how the cycle of his life might have been closed, and how, somehow, it still remains open . . .

8

SARDINIA

And so I went to Sardinia, searching for Gramsci's phantom, following the circle of his life. An hour's fight from Rome's Ciampino took me to Cagliari, Sardinia's principal city, to its small airport on the island's southernmost tip. Then I drove a little Mitsubishi rental one and a half hours northwest, chugging along a largely empty central E25 highway, battling a stiff crosswind, onward toward the twelfth-century town of Santu Lussurgiu. Santu Lussurgiu is a labyrinth of narrow cobbled streets, many scarcely wider than my tiny car. With a couple of modest supermarkets, a butcher's store, a few sad, lonely cafés, a population of around 2,500, it felt more like a large village, the sort of place where any strange car, unfamiliar to locals, provoked incredulous stares, as if an alien had landed from another planet.

I'd come excitedly to Santu Lussurgiu. I'd found inexpensive bed-and-breakfast accommodation in the same building, *Sa Murighessa*, where a teenage Gramsci lodged during his junior high school years. With its thick stone walls, wooden beamed ceilings, and granite staircase, *Sa Murighessa* today is one of a group of beautifully renovated buildings belonging to the *Antica*

Dimora de Gruccione, an "*albergo diffuso*," a special kind of traditional inn. Room and board are provided in assorted historic buildings scattered around one another (hence diffuse); an old family house typically forms the heart of the *albergo*'s hospitality, for guests' meals and collective conviviality.

Sa Murighessa has a plaque on its outside wall, memorializing Gramsci. He himself, though, remembers it as a "miserable *pensione*." "When I attended junior high school at Santu Lussurgiu," he told Tatiana (September 12, 1932), "where three professors quite brazenly made short shrift of Instruction in all five grades, I used to live in a peasant woman's house (I paid five lira a month for lodgings, bed linen, and the cooking of the very frugal board) whose old mother was a little stupid and forgetful but not crazy and was in fact my housekeeper and who every morning when

she saw me again asked me who I was and how it was that I had slept in their house."

The actual school, Ginnasio Carta-Meloni, at Via Giovanni Maria Angioi 109, was a few minutes' walk away. It no longer exists. These days, it's a private residence, smartly maintained with an ochre-colored façade, with another brown plaque on the outside wall, announcing "*I passi di Gramsci Santu Lussurgiu*" (The steps of Antonio Gramsci Santu Lussurgiu), which, in three languages (Italian, Sard, and English), says: "*Here was located the Gymnasium Carta-Meloni during Antonio Gramsci's Studies, 1905–1907.*" Underneath is a citation from *Prison Notebooks*: "Culture isn't having a well-stocked warehouse of news but is the ability that our mind has to understand life, the place we hold there, our relationship with other people. Those who are aware of themselves and of everything, who feel the relationship with all other beings, have culture. . . . So anyone can be cultured, can be a philosopher."

Gramsci hated his junior high school; they were wretched years, he said. Even as a young lad he could see through his teachers, didn't respect them, knew their inadequacies. A precocious intelligence was already manifest. In another letter to Tatiana (June 2, 1930), he writes: "One day I saw a strange little animal, like a green grass snake yet with four tiny legs. Locally, the small reptile was known as a *scurzone*, and in Sardinian dialect *curzu* means short." At school, he asked his natural history teacher what the animal was called in Italian and the teacher laughed, saying it was a *basilico*, a term used for an imaginary animal, something not real. Young Antonio must be mistaken

because what he described doesn't exist. His school chums later made fun of him, too. "You know how angry a boy can get," he tells Tatiana, "being told he is wrong when he knows instead that he is right when a question of reality is at stake; I think that it is due to this reaction against authority put to the service of self-assured ignorance that I still remember the episode." From an early age he'd developed a nose for sniffing out *authority put to the service of self-assured ignorance.*

Nino had a set routine in those school years, leaving Ghilarza early Monday morning, on a horse-drawn cart, traveling the twelve miles over the *tanca* (pastureland) on a dirt track, returning either Friday afternoon or Saturday morning, often on foot. The area could be hairy, bandit and cattle thief country. Years later he remembered an incident walking with a friend, coming back from school one Saturday morning, plodding along a deserted spot when, all of a sudden, they heard gunshots and stray bullets whistling by. Quickly they realized it was *they* who were being shot at! The duo scrambled into a ditch for cover, hugging the ground for a long while, until they were sure the coast was clear. "Obviously," he tells Tatiana, "it was a bunch of fellows out for a laugh, who enjoyed scaring us—some joke, eh! It was pitch dark when we got home, very tired and muddy, and we told nobody what had happened."

Back then, getting to and from school on foot would have taken Gramsci most of the day, even without being fired upon, and several hours by horse-drawn cart. In more modern times, on Sardinia's surprisingly smooth, well-maintained country roads, you can zip along the SP15 in a shade over twenty minutes. Though if you motor too fast, you'll miss much of what's noteworthy about the island's landscape. Not least its *stones.* John Berger is right when he says that "in the hinterland around Ghilarza, as in many parts of the island, the thing you feel most strongly is the presence of stones." "Sardinia is first and foremost a place of stones." "Endless and ageless dry-stone walls separate the *tancas*," John says, "border the gravel roads, enclose pens for the sheep, or, having fallen apart after centuries of use, suggest ruined labyrinths. Everywhere a stone is touching a stone." John reckons that stones "gave Gramsci or inspired in him his special sense of time and his special patience." Stones are silently *there*, stoic and solid, resistant to time, enduring the passage of time, unmoved, knowing that life on earth goes on over the long durée. The notion surely wasn't lost on its native radical son.

Under a blazingly hot sun, in the lizard-dry countryside before me, I could feel the presence of stones, thick basalt blocks dramatically stacked one on top of the other, forming the most archaeologically significant feature of Sardinia: *nuraghi*—tall dry-stone towers, some over forty feet high. Throughout the

island there are around 7,000 *nuraghi* remaining, important
testimonies of Sardinia's Bronze Age. *Nuraghe Losa*, on the
Abbasanta plateau, a mile or so outside Ghilarza, has an imposing central rectangular keep, surrounded by outer rings of stone
walls. It's now a UNESCO World Heritage site. Other *nuraghi*,
like *Nuraghe Zuras*, are off the beaten track, along a narrow
grassy path near the SP15. I could tell *Zuras* hadn't been visited
for some time: the grass beside it was overgrown, full of weeds;
some giant stone blocks, centuries old, had collapsed; the brown
sign, detailing the site's history, had broken away from its posting
and lay upended on the ground.

Like most *nuraghi*, *Zuras* has a single entrance, low and narrow,
with an interior staircase. *Zuras* looked so forlorn that I was reluctant to crouch and enter the pitched darkness. What lay inside?
An animal's lair? A bees' nest? Masses of cobwebs? Snakes? I
didn't fancy finding out. Nobody knows the precise function

of *nuraghi*, excepting that they weren't, like ancient Egyptian pyramids, burial grounds, places of the dead: *nuraghi* were very much structures for the living. Most likely they mixed protective and defensive activities, offering shelter to shepherds during inclement weather, and lookout posts for military surveillance; once ascended, they afford dramatic vistas across the whole countryside.

Stones figure prominently in Sardinian imagination and meant a lot to Gramsci; he'd touched many, collected many scattered around the surrounding *tanca*. At home, he spent hours with a chisel smoothing those stones down, shaping them into pairs of spheres of commensurate sizes, as big as grapefruits and melons, hollowing out little grooves inside each rock. Once ready, he'd insert into the holes pieces of a broom handle he'd cut up, foot-long lengths. He'd then join the spherical stones together, forming homemade, makeshift dumbbells. Gramsci used six stones to

make three sets of dumb-
bells of varying weights,
and with them, every
morning, as hard as he
could, as disciplined as
he was, he did exercises
to strengthen his weak
body—his arms, shoul-
ders, and back muscles,
making himself more
robust to confront the
great and terrible world
he knew lay beyond.

THE GRAMSCIS LIVED IN THE CENTER OF GHILARZA, AT
number 57 Corso Umberto I, still the town's main drag. The
house was built in the early nineteenth century, with two floors,
divided into six rooms: three on the ground floor, with an inner
courtyard, and three on the upper floor. From the age of seven
until twenty, Gramsci shared the abode with his mother, father,
and six siblings—Gennaro, Grazietta, Emma, Mario, Teresina,
and Carlo. In what would become a life of lodgings, hotel rooms,
clinics, and prison cells, the Ghilarza house was the only place
he'd ever call home, always remember affectionately; a haven
he'd return to nostalgically in his prison letters, cherishing it as
a site of Gramscian collective memory. The plain, white-walled
stone building, with a little upper-floor iron-grilled balcony, is
today fittingly preserved as *Casa Museo Antonio Gramsci*, exhib-
iting a small yet significant array of Gramsci memorabilia for
public viewing.

Months prior, I'd corresponded with the museum to arrange a
visit. They'd welcomed me, yet said: "The Casa Museo Antonio

Gramsci is closed for major restoration works. But you can visit a temporary exhibition in the premises of Piazza Gramsci, right in front of the museum house. The temporary exhibition contains a chronological journey through the life of Gramsci and preserves a large part of the objects, photos, and documents present within the museum itinerary. The exhibition is accompanied by captions in Italian and English. . . . We await your e-mail to plan your visit. See you soon!'"

And now I was parking my car along Corso Umberto I, headed for Piazza Gramsci. To the left, looking spick and span, I recognized from photographs Gramsci's old house; the adjoining properties, at numbers 59 and 61, were covered in plastic sheeting, concealing the building works going on within, the renovation of the museum complex. Almost opposite, on the other side of the street, I noticed something that would have doubtless thrilled Gramsci: the offices of a small, independent publishing house, a radical Sardinian press whose name sets the tone of its politics: *Iskra Edizioni*, after Lenin's fortnightly socialist newspaper, produced in exile in London then smuggled back into Russia where it became an influential underground paper. Iskra Edizioni, founded in Ghilarza in 2000, tries to keep alive Sardinian folk traditions and dialect, and deals with translations of academic books and reissuing of militant texts that "can no longer be found on the market."

Around the corner is Piazza Gramsci. Two young women welcomed me into the museum's makeshift store, full of everything Gramsci: tote bags and t-shirts, posters and notebooks, magazines and books, modestly for sale, all tastefully displayed. Then I was led into two temporary exhibition spaces where, left to myself, I was alone with Gramsci, overwhelmed because he was everywhere. What initially struck was his bed, a little single divan—a *very* little iron-framed divan, with two walnut wood

panels serving as the head and end boards. It was its size, its smallness, that most affected me. If Gramsci slept here until the age of twenty, you get a sense of his diminutive stature—it was like a kid's bed, not much bigger than a cot.

Nearby, a pewter washbasin and a glass cabinet containing a red and blue plaid shirt, worn by Gramsci in prison, together with toothbrush, comb, shoehorn, and shaving blade. Another glass cabinet had two grapefruit-sized stones, with two little grooves, the remains of Gramsci's dumbbells, overlaying a series of family photos, Gramsci's birth certificate, and a telegram Tatiana sent Piero Sraffa, dated April 26, 1937: "GRAMSCI COLPO APOPLETICO GRAVISSIMO, TATIANA" (GRAMSCI SUFFERED SERIOUS STROKE, TATIANA). Above it something even more disturbing: dressed in a dark suit, a photo of Gramsci on his deathbed, taken by Tatiana.

Tatiana did several things for her dead brother-in-law: besides taking care of his notebooks and arranging his burial, she had two bronze casts made, one of his right hand, his writing hand, the other a death mask, the most haunting object of all the museum's exhibits. Gramsci looks unrecognizable—bloated, with puffed up round cheeks, far removed from the youthful images of him with flowing locks of curly black hair and those famous rimless spectacles. It was a far cry indeed from how he was remembered at high school: "He may have been deformed," old school chum Renato Figari recalled, "but he wasn't ugly. He had a high forehead, with a mass of wavy hair, and behind his pince-nez I remember the bright blue of his eyes, that shining, metallic gaze, which struck you so forcibly."

Why bloated? It's difficult to say with certitude. Poor prison food? Medication for his illnesses? Sedentary life in a cell?

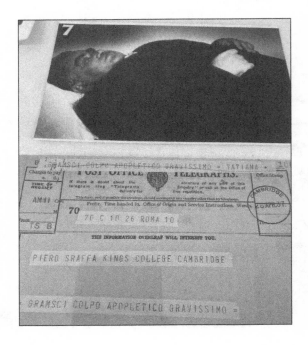

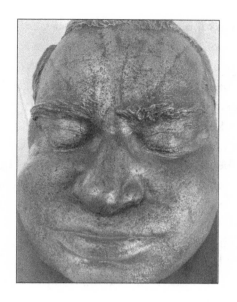

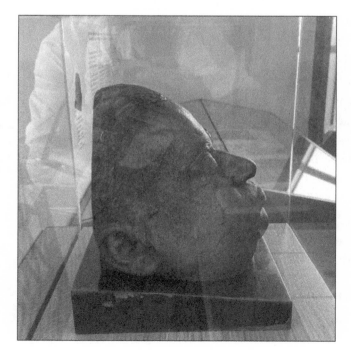

Before incarceration, Gramsci was a great walker, covering vast distances on foot, as a child and adolescent in Sardinia, and as a student in Turin, where he seemed to know old backstreets intimately. Even immediately prior to his arrest, he'd take long strolls around Rome, encountering comrades in cafés, hoofing around town to attend one meeting or another. Yet now I was looking at the cast of a man who'd aged dramatically, gained weight, and looked well beyond his forty-six years. Maybe Tatiana wanted to retain the image of her brother-in-law, whose metallic, piercing gaze was no more. Maybe she wanted to demonstrate to the world what the fascists had done to him. Lest we forget.

It was difficult not to be stirred by the exhibit, not to be affected; but I knew I had one other thing to do in Ghilarza: I had to go and see his mother, whose remains lay on the edge of town in the municipal cemetery. An attractive arched stone entrance leads you into a magnificent cypress tree paradise, aglow in gorgeous late afternoon light. Giuseppina Marcias Gramsci's grave has a prime site in the cemetery, with little around
it, marked by a horizonal
marble headstone, still
bearing the flowers of the
small commemoration of a
few weeks earlier, on April
27. A Gramsci citation is
chiseled into the foot of the
marble, words taken from a
letter he'd written his sister
Grazietta (December 29,
1930), expressing concern
about his mother's health:
"*Ha lavorato per noi tutta*

la vita, sacrificandosi in modo inaudito" (She had worked for us all her life, sacrificing herself in unimaginable ways). Gramsci's letter continues: "If she had been a different woman who knows what disastrous end we would have come to even as children; perhaps none of us would be alive today."

Over dinner that evening, back at my *albergo*, I leafed through a publication I'd picked up during my museum visit, *Mandami tante notizie di Ghilarza*. Its title is a quote from another Gramsci letter to his mother (April 25, 1927): "*Send me lots of news about Ghilarza*"; a glossy magazine produced by the Fondazione Casa Gramsci Onlus, centering on "*Paesaggi gramsciani: Il santuario campestre di San Serafino*"—Gramscian Landscapes: The Rural Sanctuary of San Serafino. San Serafino was one of his favorite boyhood stomping grounds, in a childhood much more adventurous out of school than in, a little village four miles from home, a journey Antonio would have doubtless made on foot.

The village and its chapel overlook Lake Omodeo. The lake runs into River Tirso at the Tirso River Dam and the magazine reproduces a facsimile of a postcard of the Diga del Tirso not long after its construction, one Tatiana had sent Gramsci on August 2, 1935, presumably when she was visiting his family in Ghilarza. Three other large-sized facsimiles feature in the magazine, letters Gramsci sent to his mother. One, from October 19, 1931, is worth citing at length:

> Dearest Mamma, I received your letter of the fourteenth and I was very glad to hear that you've regained your strength and that you will go for at least a day to the San Serafino festival. When I was a boy, I loved the Tirso valley below San Serafino so much! I would sit hour after hour on a rock to look at the sort of lake the river formed right below the church to watch the waterhens come out of the canebrake and swim toward the center, and the heaps of fish that were hunting mosquitos. I still remember how I once saw a large snake enter the water and come out soon after with a large eel in its mouth, and how I killed the snake and carried off the eel, which I had to throw away because it had stiffened like a stick and made my hands smell too much.

These lines told me where I needed to head next morning: to San Serafino, to another *paesaggio gramsciano*. The village was deserted when I pulled up; only a couple of languid dogs greeted me, wandering over unconcerned, not even bothering to bark, showing no signs of malice. They sniffed around me for a while, harmlessly, before lumbering back to where they came from. San Serafino village looked like a small vacation resort, shuttered up, with a series of uniform stone rowhouses, all seemingly unoccupied in non-summer months. The village's centerpiece is a

lovely chapel, pristine and somehow majestic in its understated, white-walled simplicity. Below, in the near distance, a picturesque glimpse of Gramsci's favorite lake. Herein my next mission: get to the lake, try to sit on a rock and look out as Gramsci had looked out.

I went on foot. Crossing a main road almost bereft of traffic; the signage reminded me, if I ever needed reminding, that I was in Gramsci country. At the roadside, an old hand-painted sign indicated, in yellow, "*Lago*," with an arrow pointing its direction. I followed it, descending a little gravel path. Not a soul in sight. Soon the lake came into view, Lago Omodeo, and finding a rock to sit on at the water's edge, I wondered whether I'd discovered Gramsci's actual rock, where he'd sat for hour upon hour. It was May and baking hot, 100 degrees, without shade. So I knew my visit needed to be brief, imbibing the atmosphere, getting some sense of what Gramsci experienced, of what he'd loved, and what he might have loved again.

IN TRUTH, I HAD NO REAL IDEA WHAT I WAS SEARCHING for, here or anywhere else in Sardinia. I was embarked on a peculiar research project, very *un*methodological, impossible to conceive in advance, having little inkling what I'd expect to find, let alone how I would go about trying to find it. And what was this *it* I sought anyway? I knew that part of *it* was wanting to see Gramsci's family house and museum, that I wanted to see some of the more tangible remnants of Gramsci's Sardinian world, artifacts and documents. But there were other things I was after, too, less tangible aspects of this world, more *experiential* aspects, things subjective rather than objective, sensory rather than strictly empirical. Or, at least, the sort of empirical that's hard to qualify and impossible to quantify: a smell, a texturing of the cultural and natural landscape, of Gramsci's environment, the look on people's faces, the region's light and warmth, its dusty aridness, the sun beating down, the sun setting, the sun rising, the faint ripple of the lake below San Serafino, the buzzing of insects, the sound of silence, the presence of stones.

I suppose I was accumulating *impressions*, and the impressions I'd accumulated I was now trying to recapture on the page back in Rome, where I write, reconstructing my trip from memory, realizing how much of it seemed to pass in a haze. I remember the day after San Serafino, going to Ales—I had to go to Ales (pronounced "Alice"): it was Gramsci's birthplace, after all, an hour south of Ghilarza, a town of 1,500 people that never lets you forget it is his *paese natale*; it was home only for a matter of months—the family pulled up stakes to Sorgono shortly after Antonio's birth, before permanently moving to Ghilarza. Another scorchingly hot afternoon, a fierce sun beating down. God knows how it's possible that the thermometer could rise even more in July and August. Little wonder Gramsci always felt cold in prison.

There was no shade in Ales, nowhere open, no place to eat, to buy food, to drink anything—and hot, hot, hot. Yet I was there for Gramsci, and it was endearing how much due care and attention Ales devoted to him. His actual birthplace—a two-story, yellow-façade house at Corso Cattedrale 14—is now a cultural center hosting talks, book launches, and movie showings, and still keeps the Gramscian red flag flying: one poster in the window read: "STOP ALL EMBARGO CONTRO CUBA." Gramsci's life and thought crops up everywhere in Ales, almost on every street corner, by way of a novel series of plaque-posters detailing his biographical lifeline and different aspects of his work. It had all been lovingly curated and presented, and proclaimed Ales as a "*laboratorio di idee*," a laboratory of ideas, inviting visitors "*conoscere Antonio Gramsci camminando nel suo paese natale*"—to know Antonio Gramsci by walking in his hometown.

And I did walk, headed for another landmark, another Piazza
Gramsci, with its modern stone sculpture garden that looked
weather-beaten, worn away by the sun, nicely done but utterly
deserted by day because of so little shade. As I strolled, by
chance I spotted one of the most interesting tributes to Gramsci,
an impromptu sign, unprogrammed, indicating that the man isn't

only remembered but that he's also somehow alive in people: graffiti on a rusty old door of an abandoned building, which piqued my attention and brought a smile to my face: "SONO PESSIMISTA CON INTELLIGENZA," all of which presumably implies that the daubers were somehow "*ottimista per la volontà*"— optimists of the will, as Gramsci said, summing up my own sentiment about our post-truth world.

Not far from the graffiti was the loveliest Gramsci homage I'd ever seen, the loveliest and cleverest: a giant mural painted on the whole side of a building, in bright color, huge and stunning, without any trace of desecration, sparklingly clean and vivid.

What was so interesting and clever was its blending of reality and fantasy; illustrating some of Gramsci's childhood adventures with hedgehogs, apples, and snakes; yet also showing him older, smiling, reunited with his two sons, a family portrait, a what might have been image if he'd returned to Sardinia, if Delio and Giuliano had somehow made it out of the USSR, come back to Italy to see Dad—big ifs. Where was mom Giulia? The mural was so vast that I had a hard time properly capturing it on camera.

To the uninitiated, the hedgehog-apple imagery might be perplexing. For insight let's invoke a letter (February 22, 1932) from father to son Delio:

> One autumn evening when it was already dark, but the moon was shining brightly, I went with another boy, a friend of mine, to a field full of fruit trees, especially apple trees. We hid in a bush, downwind. And there, all of a sudden, hedgehogs popped out, five of them, two larger ones and three tiny ones. In Indian file they moved toward the apple trees, wandered around in the

grass and then set to work, helping themselves with their little snouts and legs, they rolled the apples that the wind had shaken from the trees and gathered them together in a small clearing, nicely arranged close together. But obviously the apples lying on the ground were not enough; the largest hedgehog, snout in the air, looked around, picked a tree curved close to the ground and climbed up it, followed by his wife. They settled on a densely laden branch and began to swing rapidly, with brusque jolts, and many more apples fell to the ground. Having gathered these and put them next to the others, all the hedgehogs, both large and small, curled up, with their spines erect, and lay down on the apples that then were stuck to them; some had picked up only a few apples (the small hedgehogs), but father and mother had been able to pierce seven or eight apples each. As they were returning to their den, we jumped out of our hiding place, put the hedgehogs in a small sack and carried them home . . . I kept them for many months, letting them roam freely in the court-yard, they would hunt for all sorts of small animals . . . I amused myself by bringing live snakes into the courtyard to see how the hedgehogs would hunt them down.

The Ales mural offered a beautiful pictorial rendering of Gramsci's beautiful narrative tale of hedgehogs carrying apples on their backs, gathered together, about to chomp away on their harvested feast. The stars twinkle overhead, and a glowing moon gives the whole scene a magical milky charm. Gramsci, aged and portly as he was toward the end, is here radiantly alive, neatly attired in suit and tie, a proud father, arms around his two sons either side of him—*a what might have been prospect*, a Gramsci family romance, a happier epilogue to the tragic story we know really ensued.

That happy image of Gramsci disturbed me for some time.

I remember passing a morning in Santu Lussurgiu, strolling around its old center and then around what's a sort of small outer suburb, a ring of houses built sometime over the past fifty years, well after Gramsci's day. I was deep in thought about Gramsci— not about Gramsci the young lad but Gramsci the older man, the person who might have returned to walk the streets where I was walking. In olden times, Santu Lussurgiu was the site of *Sa Carrela è Nanti*, a folkloric horse race, a tradition held every Mardi Gras. Horses used to gallop through audience-flocked streets at breakneck speeds, with pairs of riders dressed in flamboyant traditional costumes, donned in obligatory Zorro-like masks. Some old town walls are decorated with framed photos of this crazy equine event, now defunct, and I looked at some showing the spectacle and its crowds as late as the 1980s.

Perched up on high in Santu Lussurgiu, where you get a sweeping vista of the whole town, is a massive white granite statue of Christ, with placating arms stretched out, and a bright red

heart that looks slightly ridiculous, like it's pulsating, beating for the salvation of the town's residents. (It resembles Jim Carrey's heart in *The Mask*, beating for Cameron Diaz.) I negotiated Santu Lussurgiu's streets, climbed upward to get a close-up of Christ, and witness that panorama before Him. All the while, I tried to visualize Gramsci back here, living in Santu Lussurgiu, imagining his niece Edmea finding Uncle Nino a room, probably near to where he used to lodge, in the old quarter, in a stone house where various relatives could come and go, cater for his needs, help him recover, regain his strength, his zest for life.

He might have taken short walks in the fresh air, got himself some false teeth, eating healthily again, found peace and quiet and maybe resumed his work, his letter writing, reconnecting with the outside world, with all the people and places he'd

formerly known. Maybe he would have taken the odd *aperi-tivo* in town, with his father Francesco, who might have lived himself had his son also lived. Gramsci Sr. and Jr. might have tippled with the townfolk; son would have enjoyed speaking their language, their dialect. It could have been right out of the leaves of Machiavelli, of Gramsci's hero's life in exile. For downtime, while working on *The Prince*, Machiavelli loved to sneak through the secret underground passageway of his Chianti wine cellar and pop up next door at a raucous tavern (*L'Albergaccio*). He'd guzzle wine, chinwag with peasants and wayfarers, play cards and exchange vulgarities with the butcher, miller, and innkeeper. "Involved in these trifles," Machiavelli said, "I kept my brain from growing moldy."

Gramsci's post-prison life might have been no less bawdy,

a homecoming dramatic and heart-wrenching, like a scene from *Cinema Paradiso*—when, after a thirty-year absence, Salvatore, the famous film director, finally returns to his native Sicilian village, attending the funeral of the old cinema projectionist, Alfredo, whom he'd adored as a kid. But maybe Gramsci's return would have been less mawkish; he wasn't one for faint-hearted nostalgia, would have probably been more hard-hearted, following the words of the island's poet laureate, Sebastiano Satta: "*His bitter heart lurches./ He does not cry:/ Sardinians should never cry.*"

On the other hand, we might wonder how long Gramsci's convalescence may have lasted before he'd gotten itchy feet, yearned for contact with the wider world again—for engaging politically again. Could he really accept, as he'd hinted to wife Giulia in 1936, "a whole cycle of his life definitively closing"? He'd spent a decade of sedentary life, within four narrow walls; it would be tough to imagine, as a free man, him wanting to sit around all day, behind a desk or in a bar, leading a quiet, meditative and contemplative existence. He'd surely have gotten bored after a while, a country boy who'd tasted the forbidden fruits of cosmopolitanism—in Turin and Vienna, in Moscow and Rome—a roving journalist, activist, and intellectual, a man who'd met Lenin and Victor Serge, who read in different languages, who'd prided himself on his internationalist outlook. Wouldn't village life have soon become too stifling, too parochial?

Another question we might pose about Gramsci's return to Sardinia: Did he really plan on staying long? Or was it just easier for him to flee Sardinia than mainland Italy—as he'd apparently told Tatiana, and as she'd written to her sister Eugenia in Moscow. A month prior to Gramsci's passing, Tatiana told Eugenia (March 25, 1937): "Antonio believes it would be a lot easier to escape from Sardinia than from Italy. We can't mention it, or rumors will start." From what would he be fleeing? The Italian fascist authorities? The Russian Communist Party and its apparatchiks, suspecting Gramsci as a closet Trotskyite? The Nazis, who'd soon be jack-booting across Europe? And where else might he go?

Gramsci never knew anything about the German bombardment of the Basque town of Guernica; it took place after he'd had his stroke, on April 26, 1937, the day prior to his death. And yet, maybe Gramsci had anticipated a darkening of Europe, was fearing the worst, knew something was brewing, that fascism was not only alive and well but would soon brazenly expand its reach, morph into Nazism. Maybe he feared what was in store for his beloved island should war break out. Mussolini saw Sardinia as a stepping-stone for enlarging his Mediterranean empire. Because of its strategic positioning—only eight miles from French Corsica—and the importance of Cagliari for launching attacks on Allied shipping in the Mediterranean, Sardinia suffered heavy bombing.

At the same time, the island also had a strong anti-fascist resistance movement, which supported the Allies, and played a significant role in eventual Italian liberation in 1943. If he'd stayed in Sardinia, what role would Gramsci have assumed? A leader of the underground resistance movement? A free man yet a communist enemy of the Nazis, a man who would need to battle on three fronts—against the German Nazis, the Italian fascists, and the Russian Stalinists. Whatever the case, it's clear his Sardinia peace would have been short-lived, lasting a couple of years only.

Would he have opted to join the dissident exodus from mainland Europe? It's fascinating to consider that the northern Sardinian port of Porto Torres had a direct ferry line to Marseille; from Porto Torres Gramsci could have traveled to the southern

French city. Although under German occupation, Marseille's shady underworld of crime and opportunism, its rowdy bars and back alleys around the Vieux Port, its seafaring and immigrant culture meant it slipped through the tightening grip of the Gestapo. The city's cracks offered illicit protection for assorted refugees, dissidents, and Jews, while becoming a wartime waystation for the passage out to the new world. (One of Gramsci's contemporaries, Walter Benjamin, born 1892, famously didn't make it out, crossing the Pyrenees from Marseille in September 1940 only to find the Spanish border closed. Stranded, without the right exit visa, he preferred suicide to being sent back, overdosing on morphine in a cheap Portbou hotel.)

Might Gramsci have sought refuge with the celebrated artists and intellectuals on the outskirts of Marseille, at the Villa Air Bel, before setting sail in March 1941 on *Le Capitaine Paul Lemerle*, a converted cargo boat, for Martinique? What a mesmerizing proposition that would have been. Onboard were 350 refugees, as well as a glitterati of creative dissidents, castaways

of old Europe, including anthropologist Claude Lévi-Strauss, photographer Germaine Krull, surrealist painter Wifredo Lam, the "Pope" of Surrealism himself, André Breton, his wife, the painter-dancer Jacqueline Lamba, together with their six-year-old daughter Aube. The anarcho-Bolshevik revolutionary Victor Serge, himself no stranger to political persecution and imprisonment, was another passenger, accompanied by his twenty-year-old son Vlady, a budding artist.

Serge and Gramsci were kindred spirits, contemporaries who knew each other in Vienna in the mid-1920s. (There's a touching photograph of them together, a group shot on a Viennese street, with optimism in the air and a grinning Gramsci.) Serge was remorselessly scathing about people he didn't like or rate—his *Notebooks, 1936–1947* are full of selected character assassinations—yet was generous about those he knew and/or admired, like Gramsci.

A few years after his arrival in Mexico, Serge wrote in his *Memoirs of a Revolutionary* perhaps the nicest portrait of Gramsci ever written:

Antonio Gramsci was living in Vienna, an industrious and Bohemian exile, late to bed and late to rise, working with the illegal committee of the Italian Communist Party. His head was heavy, his brow high and broad, his lips thin, the whole was carried on a puny, square-shouldered, weak-chested, hunchbacked body. There was grace in the movements of his fine, lanky hands. Gramsci fitted awkwardly into the humdrum of day-to-day existence, losing his way at night in familiar streets, taking the wrong train, indifferent to the comfort of his lodgings and the quality of his meals—but, intellectually, he was absolutely alive. Trained intuitively in the dialectic, quick to uncover falsehood and transfix it with the sting of irony, he viewed the world with exceptional clarity . . . a frail invalid held in both detestation and respect by Mussolini, Gramsci remained in Rome to carry on the struggle. He was fond of telling stories about his childhood; how he failed his entry into the priesthood, for which his family had marked him out. With short bursts of sardonic laughter, he exposed certain leading figures of fascism with whom he was closely acquainted . . . a fascist jail kept him outside the operation of those factional struggles whose consequence nearly everywhere was the elimination of the militants of his generation. Our years of darkness were his years of stubborn resistance.

Amid an atmosphere of fugitive uncertainty and fear—fear of being torpedoed or detained by Vichy-controlled Martinique—Serge and Gramsci would have had plenty to talk about aboard *Le Capitaine Paul Lemerle*, plenty of time to argue, to agree and disagree, to agree about disagreeing. Both had the capacity of conviction, believing in the unity of thought, energy, and life, yet were critical of all forms of fanaticism. Both knew every idea is subject to revision in the face of new realities. Both would have agreed that the old world was dying and little was left of what they'd known, of what they'd struggled for (Serge's own title for his memoirs was originally *Memories of Vanished Worlds*); both knew the new world had yet to be born and monsters lurked in the interregnum, in the darkness at dawn, in the unforgiving years they were each living out. Both would have shared prison tales of hardship and disappointment, told jokes with an inmate gallows humor they knew firsthand.

They'd have likely discussed the relative merits of anarchism and Marxism, agreed about the disasters of Stalinism, found common ground on the need to rebuild socialism through a Constituent Assembly. (In his *Notebooks*, Serge said socialists "ought to seek influence on the terrain of democracy, in the

Constituent Assemblies and elsewhere, accepting compromise in an intransigent spirit.") They'd have converged and diverged in their views about Georges Sorel, the French political theorist, agreeing about aspects of his anarcho-syndicalism, particularly on the general strike, about its "mythical" nature, that it was a "concrete fantasy" (as Gramsci called it) for arousing and organizing a collective will; yet would have disagreed about Sorel's ethical repugnance to Jacobinism, which Gramsci recognized as "the categorical embodiment of Machiavelli's *Prince*." The jury would have been out on Gramsci's feelings about Sorel's "moral elite," which Serge liked, the idea that history depends on the caliber of individuals, on how fit and capable they are for making revolution. Maybe Gramsci might have agreed; perhaps this was just another notion of an "organic intellectual."

After landing in Martinique, where might Gramsci have gone? Followed comrade Serge to Mexico? Taken André Breton's route, found refuge in New York? They never let Serge into America; no Communist Party member, existent or previous, was ever granted entry; Gramsci would have experienced a similar fate. Mexico would have been the more likely bet. Serge's weak heart didn't last long in high-altitude Mexico City: a cardiac arrest struck him down in the back of a cab in 1947. It took several hours before his body was identified. Vlady recalls finding his father on a police station slab. Son noticed the sorry state of dad's shoes, his soles full of holes, which shocked Vlady because his father had always been so careful about his appearance, even during times of worst deprivation. A few days on, Vlady sketched Dad's hands, which were, as Serge had described Gramsci's, very beautiful. Not long after, Serge's final poem was discovered, drafted the day before he'd died, called "Mains" ("Hands"): "*What astonishing contact, old man, joins your hands with ours!*"

I know, I know—all of this is idle conjecture about Gramsci,

maybe even pointless wish-
imaging. It didn't happen.
What really happened hap-
pened: Gramsci died, never
made it out, was never
reunited with Serge. While
we can act and should
speculate on the future, we
can't change the past, the
course of a history already
done. That past can be fal-
sified, erased and denied, of
course, as people in power
frequently do—remember
Gramsci's youthful article
from *Avanti!*, penned in

1917, documenting a common bourgeois trait, prevalent today,
of renaming old city streets, of coining new names for neighbor-
hoods where a working-class past was vivid. "Armed with an
encyclopedia and an ax, they proceed to demolish old Turin,"
Gramsci wrote of his adopted city. "Streets are the common heritage of people," he said, "of their affections, which united individuals more closely with the bonds of a solidarity of memory."

So we can't reinvent Gramsci's past, shouldn't reinvent that
past. But we might keep his memory alive, find solidarity in that
memory, keep him free from any renaming, from the encyclopedia and the ax. His phantom, his death mask, can haunt our present and our future. To remember what happened to him is never
to forget his dark times, the dark times that might well threaten
us again. Victor Serge recognized this, somehow knew it was his
friend's most powerful weapon. Twelve years after their Viennese
encounter, "when I emerged from a period of deportation

in Russia and arrived in Paris," Serge writes in *Memoirs of a Revolutionary*, "I was following a Popular Front demonstration when someone pushed a communist pamphlet into my hand: it contained a picture of Antonio Gramsci, who had died on April 27 of that year." What should we do with this picture in our own hands?

Remember it and pass it on.